Go Programming Language: Build Fast, Scalable Applications

Learn the Go Language for High-Performance Systems

Greyson Chesterfield

COPYRIGHT

DISCLAIMER

The information provided in this book is for general informational purposes only. All content in this book reflects the author's views and is based on their research, knowledge, and experiences. The author and publisher make no representations or warranties of any kind concerning the completeness, accuracy, reliability, suitability, or availability of the information contained herein.

This book is not intended to be a substitute for professional advice, diagnosis, or treatment. Readers should seek professional advice for any specific concerns or conditions. The author and publisher disclaim any liability or responsibility for any direct, indirect, incidental, or consequential loss or damage arising from the use of the information contained in this book.

Contents

Introduction

Why Go? A Beginner's Perspective

History of Go and Its Creators

The Go programming language, often referred to as Golang, was created in 2007 by three Google engineers: Robert Griesemer, Rob Pike, and Ken Thompson. These individuals were already well-known in the tech world, having worked on foundational projects such as UNIX and the C programming language. Go was born out of their frustration with the complexity and inefficiencies of existing programming languages for large-scale software development.

At Google, the infrastructure was sprawling, and existing languages like C++ and Java posed significant challenges in terms of build times, debugging, and scalability. The creators envisioned a language that combined the best of both worlds: the efficiency and control of low-level languages like C, and the ease of use and rapid development cycles seen in higher-level languages like Python.

Go officially launched in 2009 as an open-source project. Its creators aimed to solve three key issues:

1. **Speed:** Faster compilation and execution.

2. **Simplicity:** A minimalistic, intuitive syntax.

3. **Concurrency:** Built-in support for concurrent programming, essential for modern computing.

Key Features of Go

Go's unique blend of features has made it one of the most popular languages for modern application development. Let's break down these features with real-world implications:

1. **Simplicity**
   Go is deliberately minimalistic. It avoids bloated features found in other languages, like excessive inheritance, complex generics, or macros. This simplicity lowers the barrier for new developers and accelerates development.

   - *Example:* A junior developer can understand a Go codebase much faster compared to a complex Java or C++ application.

2. **Concurrency**
   Built-in support for goroutines and channels makes concurrent programming simple and effective. Unlike traditional threads, goroutines are lightweight and scalable, making it easy to handle tasks in parallel.

   - *Example:* A Go-based web server can handle thousands of simultaneous requests without breaking a sweat.

3. **Scalability**
   Go was designed to thrive in distributed

systems and cloud environments. Its statically typed nature ensures robust applications, while its concurrency model helps scale effortlessly.

- o *Example:* Dropbox rewrote key components of its infrastructure in Go to improve scalability and maintainability.

4. **Performance**
Go's compiled nature means that it runs at near-C speeds. At the same time, its garbage collection system ensures efficient memory management without developer intervention.

- o *Example:* Video streaming platforms like YouTube benefit from Go's ability to process high-bandwidth video streams efficiently.

Why Businesses Like Google, Netflix, and Dropbox Use Go

The adoption of Go by major tech giants highlights its relevance in solving real-world challenges:

1. **Google**
As Go's birthplace, Google uses it extensively in internal and public projects, including Kubernetes, one of the world's leading container orchestration tools. Go's performance and simplicity make it ideal for managing distributed systems at scale.

2. **Netflix**
   Netflix employs Go for its data pipeline infrastructure. The company uses Go to process and analyze massive amounts of data in real-time, ensuring seamless content delivery to millions of users globally.

3. **Dropbox**
   Dropbox transitioned from Python to Go for many of its backend services. The switch resulted in a significant reduction in server costs and improved system reliability.

4. **Uber**
   Uber leverages Go for its geofencing services. The language's low-latency capabilities ensure quick calculations for driver and rider matching.

How Go Solves Challenges in Microservices Architecture

Microservices architecture is a popular approach to software development where applications are broken into small, independent services. This architecture introduces unique challenges, including communication overhead, scalability, and debugging complexity. Go excels in addressing these challenges.

1. **Low Resource Usage**
   Go's compiled binaries are lightweight and efficient, reducing the resource footprint of

individual microservices. This is especially important in containerized environments like Kubernetes.

2. **Concurrency for Communication**
   In a microservices system, services often communicate asynchronously. Go's goroutines and channels simplify asynchronous communication, reducing bottlenecks and improving performance.

   - *Example:* A payment service can handle multiple incoming payment requests simultaneously without creating blocking threads.

3. **Ease of Deployment**
   Go's single-binary deployment model eliminates runtime dependencies. Developers can build a Go service and deploy it as a standalone executable, reducing operational complexity.

   - *Example:* A monitoring tool for microservices health checks can be built and deployed quickly.

4. **Observability and Debugging**
   Go offers robust debugging and profiling tools like pprof, which are critical for maintaining observability in microservices. Developers can monitor performance and diagnose bottlenecks effectively.

5. **Case Study: Building a Real-World Microservice**

Imagine a streaming platform like Spotify, where different services handle user authentication, playlist management, and music streaming. Using Go, the team can:

- Develop a lightweight authentication service to handle millions of login requests daily.

- Build a scalable playlist service with concurrent request handling to manage user data.

- Create a robust streaming service to deliver content with minimal latency.

Go's deliberate simplicity, combined with its powerful features, makes it an ideal choice for developers and organizations tackling modern challenges. From streamlining large-scale software at Google to powering efficient microservices at Netflix, Go stands as a testament to thoughtful language design.

This chapter has introduced you to the history, features, and real-world applications of Go. In the following chapters, we'll explore how to harness Go's capabilities to build fast, scalable applications, starting with setting up your Go environment.

Getting Started with Go

Setting Up Your Go Environment

To start coding in Go, you'll need to install it, set up your development environment, and familiarize yourself with Go's tools. This chapter walks you through each step, ensuring a smooth introduction to programming in Go.

Installing Go and Setting Up Your Workspace

1. **Downloading Go**
   To install Go, visit the official Go website and download the appropriate installer for your operating system (Windows, macOS, or Linux).

   - *Windows:* Download the .msi file and follow the installation instructions.

   - *macOS:* Use the .pkg installer.

   - *Linux:* Use the .tar.gz file and extract it to a directory like /usr/local. Add the Go binary to your $PATH.

2. **Verifying the Installation**
   After installation, open your terminal or command prompt and run:

bash

go version

You should see output indicating the installed Go version, confirming the installation was successful.

3. **Setting Up Your Workspace**
   Go organizes projects using a workspace structure. A typical workspace includes:

   - **src**: Contains source code.

   - **pkg**: Stores package object files.

   - **bin**: Stores compiled executables.

Create a directory for your workspace, for example:

bash

mkdir ~/go

Then, set the GOPATH environment variable to point to this directory:

   - *Linux/macOS:* Add the following to your .bashrc or .zshrc file:

bash

export GOPATH=~/go

export PATH=$PATH:$GOPATH/bin

○ *Windows:* Add GOPATH as a system environment variable.

Introduction to Go Tools

Go comes with a suite of powerful tools that simplify coding, building, and running applications. Let's explore the most commonly used tools.

1. **go run**
   This command compiles and executes your code in one step, perfect for quick testing during development.

   ○ *Example:*
   Save the following code in a file named main.go:

```go
go
```

```go
package main


import "fmt"


func main() {
    fmt.Println("Hello, Go!")
}
```

Run it with:

bash

go run main.go

Output:

Hello, Go!

2. **go build**
   This command compiles your code into a
   standalone binary executable. It's useful for
   production-ready applications.

   - *Example:*
     Run:

bash

go build main.go

This will create an executable (main on Linux/macOS
or main.exe on Windows) in the same directory.
Execute it directly to see the output.

3. **go mod**
   The go mod tool manages dependencies using
   Go modules. Modules are collections of related
   Go packages.

   - *Initialize a module:*

bash

```bash
go mod init myproject
```

This creates a go.mod file in your project directory, which tracks dependencies.

- *Add a dependency:*
  Use go get to fetch a package:

```bash
bash
```

```bash
go get github.com/gin-gonic/gin
```

The go.mod file will automatically update to include the dependency.

Your First Go Program: "Hello, World"

Now that your environment is set up, let's write your first program in Go and understand it step by step.

1. **Creating the Program**
   Open your text editor or IDE and create a file named main.go with the following content:

```go
go
```

```go
package main
```

```go
import "fmt"
```

```go
func main() {

    fmt.Println("Hello, World!")

}
```

2. **Understanding the Code**
   Let's break it down:

   - **package main:**
     Every Go program starts with a package declaration. The main package is special—it defines the entry point of the application.

   - **import "fmt":**
     The fmt package provides formatted I/O functions. Here, we use it to print text to the console.

   - **func main() { ... }:**
     The main() function is the starting point of execution for Go programs.

3. **Running the Program**
   Use the go run command to execute your program:

bash

```bash
go run main.go
```

Output:

Hello, World!

4. **Compiling the Program**
   To compile your program into a binary, use go build:

bash

go build main.go

Run the resulting executable to see the same output.

Troubleshooting Common Issues

1. **Go Command Not Found**
   If running go version or go run gives an error, double-check that Go is installed correctly and that the binary path is added to your PATH environment variable.

2. **Cannot Find Package**
   This error occurs if you try to import a package that isn't installed or isn't in your module. Use go mod tidy to clean up and resolve dependencies.

3. **Permission Errors**
   Ensure you have write access to your workspace directory or use a directory where you have the appropriate permissions.

Experimenting Further

To gain confidence with Go tools and the language, try these mini-projects:

1. **Simple Arithmetic Calculator**
   Write a program that takes two numbers and an operator (+, -, *, /) as input and outputs the result.

2. **File Reader**
   Create a Go program to read a text file and display its contents line by line.

3. **Goroutine Example**
   Experiment with concurrency by creating a program that runs two goroutines to print messages simultaneously.

By now, you should have Go installed and your workspace ready. You've also explored Go's essential tools (go run, go build, go mod) and written your first Go program. These foundational skills set the stage for deeper exploration into Go's powerful features in the coming chapters. Next, we'll dive into Go's basics, including variables, constants, and data types.

Understanding Go Basics

Programming in Go revolves around understanding its foundational building blocks: variables, constants, and data types. These elements provide the tools to store, manipulate, and interact with data in meaningful ways. In this chapter, we'll explore these concepts with practical examples, including creating a basic calculator.

Variables in Go

Variables in Go are used to store data that can change during the program's execution. Let's break down how they work.

1. **Declaring Variables**
   Go offers several ways to declare variables:

   o **Explicit Declaration:**

go

var a int

a = 5

Here, a is declared as an integer and later assigned a value.

- ○ **Short Declaration (Preferred for simplicity):**

go

```
b := 10
```

This declares and initializes b in one step. Go infers the type based on the value assigned.

2. **Multiple Declarations**
   You can declare multiple variables at once:

go

```
var x, y, z int = 1, 2, 3
```

3. **Zero Values**
   Uninitialized variables are automatically assigned a "zero value":

   - ○ Numbers: 0

   - ○ Strings: ""

   - ○ Booleans: false

   - ○ Pointers: nil

Example:

go

```go
var n int

fmt.Println(n) // Outputs: 0
```

4. **Real-World Example: Bank Account Balance**
   Let's write a simple program to track a bank account balance:

```go
package main

import "fmt"

func main() {
    var balance float64 = 100.50
    deposit := 50.25
    balance += deposit
    fmt.Printf("Updated balance: $%.2f\n", balance)
}
```

Constants in Go

Constants are similar to variables but cannot be changed once declared. Use constants for values that remain fixed throughout the program.

1. **Declaring Constants**

```go
go
```

```go
const pi = 3.14159

const name string = "Go Programming"
```

2. **Enumerated Constants**
   Using iota, you can create sequences:

```go
go
```

```go
const (

    Small = iota

    Medium

    Large

)

fmt.Println(Small, Medium, Large) // Outputs: 0 1 2
```

3. **Real-World Example: Tax Calculator**
   Let's calculate the total cost of a product
   including a constant tax rate:

```go
go
```

```go
package main

import "fmt"
```

```go
const taxRate = 0.07 // 7%

func main() {
    price := 100.00
    total := price + (price * taxRate)
    fmt.Printf("Total cost: $%.2f\n", total)
}
```

Data Types in Go

Go provides several data types, which can be broadly categorized into the following groups:

1. **Basic Types**
   - **Numbers:**
     - Integers (int, int8, uint32, etc.)
     - Floating-point numbers (float32, float64)
     - Example:

go

```go
var age int = 30
var temperature float64 = 36.6
```

- o **Strings:**
  Strings are immutable sequences of characters.
  Example:

```go
go
```

```go
name := "Alice"

fmt.Println("Hello, " + name)
```

- o **Booleans:**
  Represent true or false values.
  Example:

```go
go
```

```go
isAdult := true

fmt.Println("Is adult?", isAdult)
```

2. **Composite Types**

- o **Arrays:** Fixed-length collections of elements of the same type.
  Example:

```go
go
```

```go
var numbers [5]int = [5]int{1, 2, 3, 4, 5}

fmt.Println(numbers)
```

- o **Slices:** Flexible and more commonly used than arrays.
  Example:

go

```go
numbers := []int{1, 2, 3}
numbers = append(numbers, 4)
fmt.Println(numbers)
```

- o **Maps:** Key-value pairs.
  Example:

go

```go
scores := map[string]int{"Alice": 90, "Bob": 80}
fmt.Println(scores["Alice"])
```

- o **Structs:** Custom data types that group related fields.
  Example:

go

```go
type Person struct {
    Name string
    Age  int
}
```

```go
person := Person{Name: "Alice", Age: 30}

fmt.Println(person)
```

Creating a Basic Calculator

Let's apply what we've learned to create a simple calculator that performs addition, subtraction, multiplication, and division.

1. **Calculator Program**

go

```go
package main

import "fmt"

func main() {
    var num1, num2 float64
    var operator string

    fmt.Println("Enter the first number:")
    fmt.Scanln(&num1)

    fmt.Println("Enter the second number:")
```

```go
    fmt.Scanln(&num2)

    fmt.Println("Enter an operator (+, -, *, /):")
    fmt.Scanln(&operator)

    switch operator {
    case "+":
        fmt.Printf("Result: %.2f\n", num1+num2)
    case "-":
        fmt.Printf("Result: %.2f\n", num1-num2)
    case "*":
        fmt.Printf("Result: %.2f\n", num1*num2)
    case "/":
        if num2 != 0 {
            fmt.Printf("Result: %.2f\n", num1/num2)
        } else {
            fmt.Println("Error: Division by zero is not allowed.")
        }
    default:
        fmt.Println("Invalid operator. Please use +, -, *, or /.")
    }
```

}

2. **Explanation**

- **Input Handling:** The fmt.ScanIn function captures user input for numbers and the operator.

- **Switch Case:** The switch statement evaluates the operator and performs the corresponding calculation.

- **Division Check:** A safeguard ensures division by zero is avoided.

3. **Sample Run**
Input:

mathematica

Enter the first number:

10

Enter the second number:

5

Enter an operator (+, -, *, /):

*

Output:

makefile

Result: 50.00

Common Pitfalls and Best Practices

1. **Avoid Unused Variables**
   Go does not allow declaring variables without using them. This feature encourages clean, meaningful code.

```go
go
```

var x int // Error: x is declared but not used

2. **Type Mismatch**
   Ensure you perform operations on variables of compatible types.

```go
go
```

var x int = 10

var y float64 = 5.5

// z := x + y // Error: mismatched types

3. **Use Constants Where Appropriate**
   Replace magic numbers with constants to improve readability and maintainability:

```go
go
```

```
const discountRate = 0.1
```

This chapter introduced variables, constants, and data types in Go, along with their practical applications. Through a real-world example of a basic calculator, you saw how these building blocks come together to form functional programs. Mastery of these fundamentals sets the foundation for more advanced topics, such as control flow and error handling, which we'll explore next.

Go's Unique Syntax

Go's syntax is one of its defining features. It's designed to be simple, clean, and readable, making it approachable for beginners while remaining powerful enough for advanced developers. This chapter explores Go's structure and simplicity, and we'll implement a practical example: a CLI tool for renaming files.

Exploring Go's Structure

Go's syntax prioritizes clarity and eliminates unnecessary complexity. Here are some of its structural highlights:

1. **Minimalist Approach**
   Go avoids features like classes, inheritance, or extensive operator overloading, focusing instead on straightforward functionality. Example: Instead of classes, Go uses structs and interfaces.

2. **Standard Formatting with gofmt**
   Go enforces a consistent coding style through the gofmt tool, which automatically formats code. This eliminates debates over styling and ensures uniformity.

3. **Built-In Concurrency**
   Features like goroutines and channels are seamlessly integrated into the syntax, making concurrent programming simple.

4. **Package-Based Organization**
   All Go programs are organized into packages, promoting modularity. Every program starts with a main package, which serves as the entry point.

Key Syntax Features

1. **Package Declaration**
   Every Go file begins with a package declaration. The main package is special because it defines the entry point of the program.
   Example:

go

```
package main

import "fmt"

func main() {
    fmt.Println("Welcome to Go!")
```

```go
}
```

2. **Imports**
   The import keyword brings in standard or third-party libraries. Go ensures unused imports are flagged as errors to maintain clean code.
   Example:

go

```go
import (
    "fmt"
    "os"
)
```

3. **Functions**
   Functions are central to Go programming. The main() function is the starting point.
   Example:

go

```go
func greet(name string) string {
    return "Hello, " + name
}

func main() {
    message := greet("Alice")
```

```go
    fmt.Println(message)
}
```

4. **Error Handling**
   Go uses explicit error handling instead of
   exceptions, encouraging developers to handle
   errors directly.
   Example:

```go

file, err := os.Open("example.txt")

if err != nil {

    fmt.Println("Error:", err)

    return

}

defer file.Close()
```

A Practical Example: Building a CLI Tool for File Renaming

Let's use Go's syntax and simplicity to create a
command-line tool that renames files in a directory.

Step 1: Defining the Problem

The CLI tool will:

1. Accept a directory path and a file extension as inputs.

2. Rename all files with the specified extension, appending a prefix like renamed_ to their names.

Step 2: Designing the Solution

1. Use os and filepath packages for file operations.

2. Read files in the specified directory.

3. Rename files matching the specified extension.

4. Use clear, concise syntax for error handling.

Step 3: Writing the Code

Here's the complete implementation:

go

```
package main

import (
    "fmt"
    "os"
    "path/filepath"
```

```go
        "strings"
)


func main() {
        // Step 1: Collect user inputs
        if len(os.Args) != 3 {
                fmt.Println("Usage: rename <directory> <file-extension>")
                return
        }

        directory := os.Args[1]
        extension := os.Args[2]

        // Step 2: Open the directory
        files, err := os.ReadDir(directory)
        if err != nil {
                fmt.Println("Error reading directory:", err)
                return
        }

        // Step 3: Iterate over files
```

```go
    for _, file := range files {
        if !file.IsDir() &&
strings.HasSuffix(file.Name(), extension) {
            // Step 4: Construct new file
name
            oldPath := filepath.Join(directory,
file.Name())
            newName := "renamed_" +
file.Name()
            newPath :=
filepath.Join(directory, newName)

            // Step 5: Rename the file
            err := os.Rename(oldPath,
newPath)
            if err != nil {
                fmt.Println("Error renaming
file:", file.Name(), "-", err)
                continue
            }

            fmt.Println("Renamed:",
file.Name(), "to", newName)
        }
    }
```

```
}
```

Step 4: Understanding the Code

1. **Input Handling**
   The program uses os.Args to capture
   command-line arguments. If the user doesn't
   provide the correct inputs, the program
   displays a usage message.

2. **Directory Reading**
   The os.ReadDir function lists all files in the
   specified directory. The program checks each
   file to ensure it's not a subdirectory and
   matches the desired file extension.

3. **File Renaming**
   The os.Rename function renames files. The
   filepath.Join function constructs paths in a
   platform-independent manner.

4. **Error Handling**
   Errors are explicitly checked at each stage,
   ensuring robust execution.

Step 5: Running the Tool

1. **Save the Code**
   Save the program in a file named rename.go.

2. **Build the Executable**
   Use go build to create an executable:

bash

```
go build rename.go
```

3. **Run the Program**
   Run the tool with a directory path and file
   extension as arguments:

bash

```
./rename ./testdir .txt
```

4. **Output Example**

vbnet

```
Renamed: file1.txt to renamed_file1.txt

Renamed: file2.txt to renamed_file2.txt
```

Step 6: Extending the Tool

You can extend this tool with additional features:

1. **Interactive Mode:** Prompt the user for
   confirmation before renaming files.

2. **Recursive Directory Traversal:** Rename files
   in subdirectories using filepath.WalkDir.

3. **Logging:** Save a log of renamed files for audit purposes.

Advantages of Go's Syntax for CLI Tools

1. **Simplicity:** Go's syntax is easy to read and write, even for complex tasks.

2. **Standard Library:** Built-in packages like os and filepath simplify file operations.

3. **Error Handling:** Explicit error checks make programs more predictable and robust.

4. **Cross-Platform:** Compiled Go binaries work seamlessly across operating systems.

This chapter demonstrated Go's unique syntax through the development of a practical CLI tool for file renaming. You've seen how Go's structure encourages simplicity and robustness, making it ideal for building tools and applications. Next, we'll explore functions, packages, and modules to learn how to organize and reuse code effectively.

Deep Dive into Core Concepts

Functions, Packages, and Modules in Go

Reusable, modular code is a cornerstone of maintainable software development. Go excels in promoting this with its well-defined functions, packages, and modules. In this chapter, you'll learn how to write reusable code and organize it effectively, culminating in the creation of a modular blogging tool.

Functions: The Building Blocks of Reusability

Functions in Go allow you to encapsulate logic into named blocks, promoting code reuse and readability.

Defining Functions

A function in Go has the following structure:

go

```
func functionName(parameters) returnType {
    // Function body
}
```

- **Parameters:** Input values the function uses.

- **Return Type:** Specifies the output of the function.

Example:

go

```go
func add(a int, b int) int {
    return a + b
}
```

Calling Functions

Functions are called by their name, passing arguments for the parameters:

go

```go
result := add(2, 3)
fmt.Println(result) // Outputs: 5
```

Multiple Return Values

Go supports multiple return values, often used for returning results and errors.

go

```go
func divide(a, b int) (int, error) {
    if b == 0 {
        return 0, fmt.Errorf("division by zero")
```

```go
    }
    return a / b, nil
}
```

Usage:

```go
result, err := divide(10, 2)
if err != nil {
    fmt.Println("Error:", err)
} else {
    fmt.Println("Result:", result)
}
```

Packages: Organizing Code

Packages in Go group related code together. The standard library itself is composed of packages like fmt, os, and net/http.

Creating a Package

1. **Directory Structure**
   Create a directory structure for your package:

```go

```

myproject/

├── main.go

├── mathutils/

| └── mathutils.go

2. **Package Declaration**
   In mathutils/mathutils.go:

```go


package mathutils


func Add(a, b int) int {

    return a + b

}
```

3. **Importing the Package**
   In main.go:

```go


package main


import (

    "fmt"
```

```go
    "myproject/mathutils"
)


func main() {
    result := mathutils.Add(5, 7)
    fmt.Println("Sum:", result)
}
```

Exported vs. Unexported Identifiers

- Identifiers (functions, variables, etc.) starting with an uppercase letter are exported and accessible outside the package.

- Identifiers starting with a lowercase letter are unexported and private to the package.

Modules: Dependency Management

Modules in Go allow you to manage dependencies for your project and ensure version control.

Creating a Module

1. **Initialize a Module**
   Inside your project directory, run:

bash

```
go mod init myproject
```

This creates a go.mod file:

```go
```

```
module myproject
```

```
go 1.20
```

2. **Adding Dependencies**
   Use go get to add external packages:

```bash
```

```
go get github.com/gin-gonic/gin
```

This updates the go.mod file to include the dependency.

3. **Tidying Up Dependencies**
   Use go mod tidy to clean up unused dependencies.

Using External Modules

Once a dependency is added, you can import it in your code:

```go
```

```
package main
```

```go
import (

    "fmt"

    "github.com/gin-gonic/gin"

)


func main() {

    fmt.Println("Gin framework imported!")

}
```

Project Example: Building a Modular Blogging Tool

Let's create a blogging tool to demonstrate functions, packages, and modules in action.

Step 1: Define the Project Structure

go

```
bloggingtool/

├── go.mod

├── main.go
```

```
├── posts/
│   ├── post.go
│   └── manager.go
├── utils/
│   └── formatter.go
```

Step 2: Implement the Code

1. **Posts Package**

   - posts/post.go: Define the structure of a blog post.

go

```go
package posts

type Post struct {
    ID      int
    Title   string
    Content string
}
```

   - posts/manager.go: Manage blog posts.

go

```go
package posts

import "fmt"

var posts []Post
var nextID = 1

func CreatePost(title, content string) Post {
    post := Post{
        ID:      nextID,
        Title:   title,
        Content: content,
    }
    nextID++
    posts = append(posts, post)
    return post
}

func ListPosts() {
    for _, post := range posts {
        fmt.Printf("ID: %d, Title: %s\n", post.ID,
post.Title)
```

```
    }
}
```

2. **Utils Package**

- o utils/formatter.go: Provide utility
  functions for formatting.

go

```go
package utils

import "strings"

func FormatTitle(title string) string {
    return strings.ToUpper(title)
}
```

3. **Main Program**

- o main.go: Bring it all together.

go

```go
package main

import (
    "bloggingtool/posts"
```

```go
    "bloggingtool/utils"

    "fmt"
)


func main() {

    fmt.Println("Welcome to the Blogging Tool!")


    // Create and list posts

    post1 := posts.CreatePost(utils.FormatTitle("First
Post"), "This is the first blog post.")

    post2 := posts.CreatePost(utils.FormatTitle("Go
Language"), "Learning Go is fun!")


    fmt.Println("Created posts:")

    fmt.Printf("Post 1: %v\n", post1)

    fmt.Printf("Post 2: %v\n", post2)


    fmt.Println("\nListing all posts:")

    posts.ListPosts()
}
```

Step 3: Running the Project

1. **Initialize the Module**
   Run the following in the project directory:

bash

```
go mod init bloggingtool
```

2. **Run the Program**
   Execute the program:

bash

```
go run main.go
```

3. **Expected Output**

kotlin

```
Welcome to the Blogging Tool!

Created posts:

Post 1: {1 FIRST POST This is the first blog post.}

Post 2: {2 GO LANGUAGE Learning Go is fun!}


Listing all posts:

ID: 1, Title: FIRST POST

ID: 2, Title: GO LANGUAGE
```

Step 4: Extending the Tool

Here are a few ways to extend the blogging tool:

1. **Edit and Delete Posts:** Add functions in the posts package to update and delete posts by ID.

2. **Persist Data:** Use a database like SQLite to save and retrieve posts.

3. **REST API:** Add a web interface using the net/http or gin package to make the tool accessible through HTTP.

Advantages of Functions, Packages, and Modules in Go

1. **Reusability:** Functions and packages allow you to encapsulate logic and reuse it across projects.

2. **Modularity:** Packages help organize code, making it easier to navigate and maintain.

3. **Scalability:** Modules simplify dependency management, ensuring projects scale smoothly with external libraries.

This chapter demonstrated how Go's functions, packages, and modules work together to create reusable, modular, and scalable code. By building a blogging tool, you've seen these concepts in action. In the next chapter, we'll delve into control flow and error handling, which are critical for building robust applications.

Control Flow and Error Handling in Go

Effective control flow and robust error handling are fundamental for building resilient applications. Go offers powerful constructs like loops, conditionals, and explicit error handling mechanisms (defer, panic, recover) that enable developers to write predictable and maintainable code. In this chapter, we'll explore these features through a real-world application: a resilient data parser.

Control Flow in Go

Control flow determines the sequence in which instructions are executed. Go supports essential constructs like loops and conditionals.

Conditionals

1. **if Statements** Go's if statements don't require parentheses, promoting clean syntax.

go

```
if age > 18 {
    fmt.Println("Adult")
```

```go
} else {
    fmt.Println("Minor")
}
```

2. **if with Initialization** Initialization within if is a concise way to declare variables locally.

go

```go
if score := 85; score >= 90 {
    fmt.Println("Grade: A")
} else if score >= 75 {
    fmt.Println("Grade: B")
} else {
    fmt.Println("Grade: C")
}
```

3. **switch Statements** Go's switch is more flexible than in many other languages. It doesn't require explicit break statements to avoid fallthrough.

go

```go
switch day := "Monday"; day {
case "Monday", "Tuesday":
    fmt.Println("Weekday")
```

```go
case "Saturday", "Sunday":

    fmt.Println("Weekend")
default:

    fmt.Println("Invalid day")

}
```

Loops

Go supports only the for loop, which simplifies syntax without sacrificing functionality.

1. **Basic for Loop**

go

```go
for i := 0; i < 5; i++ {

    fmt.Println(i)

}
```

2. **for as a while Loop** Omitting initialization and increment makes it a while loop:

go

```go
count := 0
for count < 5 {

    fmt.Println(count)

    count++
```

}

3. **Infinite Loops** An infinite loop is created by omitting all parts of the for statement:

go

```go
for {
    fmt.Println("Running indefinitely")
}
```

4. **Iterating Over Collections** Use the range keyword for arrays, slices, maps, or strings:

go

```go
fruits := []string{"apple", "banana", "cherry"}
for index, fruit := range fruits {
    fmt.Printf("%d: %s\n", index, fruit)
}
```

Error Handling in Go

Unlike many languages that rely on exceptions, Go uses explicit error handling, encouraging developers to address errors as they occur.

Using error Type

1. **Returning Errors** Functions return errors as part of their signature.

go

```go
func divide(a, b int) (int, error) {
    if b == 0 {
        return 0, fmt.Errorf("division by zero")
    }
    return a / b, nil
}
```

2. **Handling Errors** Errors must be explicitly checked:

go

```go
result, err := divide(10, 0)
if err != nil {
    fmt.Println("Error:", err)
} else {
    fmt.Println("Result:", result)
}
```

Defer, Panic, and Recover

1. **defer**

- Schedules a function to execute when the surrounding function returns.
- Commonly used for cleanup tasks like closing files.

go

```go
func readFile(filename string) {
    file, err := os.Open(filename)
    if err != nil {
        fmt.Println("Error:", err)
        return
    }
    defer file.Close()

    fmt.Println("File opened successfully")
}
```

2. **panic**

- Stops the program execution when a critical error occurs.
- Use sparingly for unrecoverable errors.

go

```go
func dividePanic(a, b int) int {
```

```go
    if b == 0 {
        panic("division by zero")
    }
    return a / b
}
```

   3. **recover**

   o Allows recovery from a panic to continue program execution.

go

```go
func safeDivide(a, b int) {
    defer func() {
        if r := recover(); r != nil {
            fmt.Println("Recovered from panic:", r)
        }
    }()
    fmt.Println("Result:", dividePanic(a, b))
}
```

Real-World Application: Writing a Data Parser with Error Resilience

Let's build a data parser that reads a file containing key-value pairs, validates the data, and handles errors gracefully.

Step 1: Define the Problem

The parser will:

1. Read a file with key-value pairs (e.g., data.txt):

makefile

name=John

age=30

invalid_entry

city=New York

2. Skip invalid entries and report errors without crashing.

3. Use defer, panic, and recover for cleanup and resilience.

Step 2: Plan the Solution

1. Open the file and handle potential errors.

2. Parse each line, validating the format (key=value).

3. Log invalid entries and continue processing.

Step 3: Implement the Code

Here's the complete implementation:

go

```go
package main

import (
	"bufio"
	"fmt"
	"os"
	"strings"
)

func main() {
	parseFile("data.txt")
}

func parseFile(filename string) {
```

```go
file, err := os.Open(filename)
if err != nil {
        fmt.Println("Error opening file:", err)
        return
}
defer file.Close()

scanner := bufio.NewScanner(file)
lineNumber := 0

for scanner.Scan() {
        lineNumber++
        line := scanner.Text()

        // Attempt to parse the line
        defer handleParseError(lineNumber, line)

        parseLine(line)
}

if err := scanner.Err(); err != nil {
        fmt.Println("Error reading file:", err)
}
```

```go
        }
}

func parseLine(line string) {
        // Check for valid format
        if !strings.Contains(line, "=") {
                panic("invalid format")
        }

        parts := strings.Split(line, "=")
        if len(parts) != 2 {
                panic("invalid key-value pair")
        }

        key := strings.TrimSpace(parts[0])
        value := strings.TrimSpace(parts[1])

        fmt.Printf("Parsed: %s = %s\n", key, value)
}

func handleParseError(lineNumber int, line string) {
        if r := recover(); r != nil {
```

```
        fmt.Printf("Error parsing line %d (%s):
%v\n", lineNumber, line, r)

     }

}
```

Step 4: Understanding the Code

1. **File Reading**
   The os.Open function opens the file, and
   bufio.Scanner reads it line by line.

2. **Error Handling with defer and recover**
   The handleParseError function recovers from
   panic, logging the error and allowing the
   program to continue parsing subsequent lines.

3. **Data Parsing**
   The parseLine function validates the key=value
   format. Invalid entries trigger a panic.

Step 5: Running the Program

1. **Input File (data.txt)**

makefile

name=John

age=30

invalid_entry
```
```

city=New York

2. **Run the Program**

bash

go run main.go

3. **Output**

vbnet

Parsed: name = John

Parsed: age = 30

Error parsing line 3 (invalid_entry): invalid format

Parsed: city = New York

Extending the Parser

1. **Enhanced Validation**
   Validate keys and values for specific formats
   (e.g., age must be numeric).

2. **Error Logging**
   Write errors to a separate log file instead of
   printing them to the console.

3. **Concurrent Parsing**
   Use goroutines and channels to parse large
   files concurrently.

In this chapter, you learned how Go's control flow constructs and error-handling mechanisms (defer, panic, recover) empower developers to write robust programs. Through the data parser example, you saw how to gracefully handle errors without disrupting execution. In the next chapter, we'll delve into structs, methods, and interfaces to explore Go's approach to object-like programming.

Structs, Methods, and Interfaces in Go

Go does not have traditional object-oriented programming features like classes or inheritance. Instead, it provides structs, methods, and interfaces to achieve object-like behavior. These constructs allow for powerful and flexible design patterns that emphasize composition over inheritance. In this chapter, we'll explore how to use these features and build a practical customer management system.

Structs: Custom Data Types

A struct in Go is a composite data type that groups related fields. Think of it as a blueprint for defining objects.

Defining and Using Structs

1. **Defining a Struct**

go

```
type Customer struct {
    ID    int
    Name  string
```

    Email string

}

2. **Creating Instances** You can create an
   instance of a struct in multiple ways:

   ○ Using field names:

```go
customer := Customer{ID: 1, Name: "Alice", Email: "alice@example.com"}
```

   ○ Omitting field names (values must be in order):

```go
customer := Customer{1, "Alice", "alice@example.com"}
```

   ○ Using the zero value:

```go
var customer Customer
customer.ID = 1
customer.Name = "Alice"
customer.Email = "alice@example.com"
```

3. **Accessing and Modifying Fields** Fields are accessed and modified using the dot (.) operator:

go

```
fmt.Println(customer.Name) // Outputs: Alice

customer.Email = "newemail@example.com"
```

Structs with Nested Fields

Structs can be nested to create more complex data models:

go

```
type Address struct {
    Street string
    City   string
    Zip    string
}


type Customer struct {
    ID      int
    Name    string
    Email   string
    Address Address
```

}

Usage:

```go

customer := Customer{
    ID:    1,
    Name:  "Alice",
    Email: "alice@example.com",
    Address: Address{
        Street: "123 Main St",
        City:   "New York",
        Zip:    "10001",
    },
}
fmt.Println(customer.Address.City) // Outputs: New York
```

Methods: Functions Associated with Structs

Methods in Go are functions with a receiver. They provide struct-specific behavior.

Defining Methods

```go
func (c Customer) DisplayInfo() {

    fmt.Printf("Customer ID: %d, Name: %s, Email: %s\n", c.ID, c.Name, c.Email)

}
```

- **Receiver:** (c Customer) is the receiver, making the method specific to the Customer struct.
- **Call:** Methods are called using the dot operator:

```go
customer.DisplayInfo()
```

Pointer Receivers

When modifying a struct, use a pointer receiver to avoid copying:

```go
func (c *Customer) UpdateEmail(newEmail string) {

    c.Email = newEmail

}
```

Usage:

```go
```

```
customer.UpdateEmail("updated@example.com")
```

Interfaces: Defining Behavior

An interface in Go defines a set of method signatures. Any type that implements these methods is said to satisfy the interface.

Defining and Using Interfaces

    1. **Defining an Interface**

go

```
type Notifier interface {

    Notify() string

}
```

    2. **Implementing the Interface** Any type that implements all methods in an interface satisfies it:

go

```
func (c Customer) Notify() string {

    return "Notification sent to " + c.Email

}
```

3. **Using the Interface** Interfaces enable polymorphism:

go

```go
func SendNotification(n Notifier) {
    fmt.Println(n.Notify())
}
```

Usage:

go

```go
SendNotification(customer)
```

Empty Interface

The empty interface (interface{}) can represent any type, but its use should be limited to cases where type assertions are necessary.

Example: Designing a Customer Management System

Let's combine structs, methods, and interfaces to build a customer management system.

Step 1: Define the Problem

The system will:

1. Store customer data (ID, name, email, address).

2. Allow customers to update their email addresses.

3. Notify customers of updates using an interface.

4. List all customers.

Step 2: Plan the Solution

1. Define the Customer struct and Notifier interface.

2. Implement methods for customer updates and notifications.

3. Create a slice to manage a list of customers.

Step 3: Implement the Code

Here's the full implementation:

go

```
package main

import (
        "fmt"
```

```go
)

// Address struct represents a customer's address
type Address struct {
	Street string
	City   string
	Zip    string
}

// Customer struct represents a customer
type Customer struct {
	ID      int
	Name    string
	Email   string
	Address Address
}

// Notifier interface defines a notification method
type Notifier interface {
	Notify() string
}
```

```go
// Notify sends a notification to the customer
func (c Customer) Notify() string {
        return "Notification sent to " + c.Email
}


// UpdateEmail updates the customer's email
func (c *Customer) UpdateEmail(newEmail string) {
        c.Email = newEmail
}


// CustomerManager manages a list of customers
type CustomerManager struct {
        customers []Customer
}


// AddCustomer adds a new customer to the manager
func (cm *CustomerManager) AddCustomer(customer
Customer) {
        cm.customers = append(cm.customers,
customer)
}


// ListCustomers lists all customers
```

```go
func (cm CustomerManager) ListCustomers() {
	for _, customer := range cm.customers {
		fmt.Printf("ID: %d, Name: %s, Email: %s\n", customer.ID, customer.Name, customer.Email)
	}
}


func main() {
	// Initialize customer manager
	manager := CustomerManager{}

	// Create customers
	customer1 := Customer{
		ID:    1,
		Name:  "Alice",
		Email: "alice@example.com",
		Address: Address{
			Street: "123 Main St",
			City:   "New York",
			Zip:    "10001",
		},
	}
```

```go
customer2 := Customer{
        ID:   2,
        Name:  "Bob",
        Email: "bob@example.com",
        Address: Address{
                Street: "456 Elm St",
                City:   "Los Angeles",
                Zip:    "90001",
        },
}

// Add customers to manager
manager.AddCustomer(customer1)
manager.AddCustomer(customer2)

// List customers
fmt.Println("Customer List:")
manager.ListCustomers()

// Update email for a customer
fmt.Println("\nUpdating Alice's email...")
```

```go
        customer1.UpdateEmail("alice.new@example.
com")


        // Notify customer

        fmt.Println("\nSending notification to Alice:")

        fmt.Println(customer1.Notify())

}
```

Step 4: Run the Program

1. **Save the Code**
   Save the program as customer_manager.go.

2. **Run the Program**

bash

```
go run customer_manager.go
```

3. **Output**

yaml

```
Customer List:
ID: 1, Name: Alice, Email: alice@example.com
ID: 2, Name: Bob, Email: bob@example.com


Updating Alice's email...
```

Sending notification to Alice:

Notification sent to alice.new@example.com

Step 5: Extend the System

1. **Search by ID**
   Add a method to find a customer by ID.

go

```go
func (cm CustomerManager) FindCustomerByID(id int) *Customer {
    for _, customer := range cm.customers {
        if customer.ID == id {
            return &customer
        }
    }
    return nil
}
```

2. **Delete Customers**
   Implement a method to remove customers by ID.

3. **Persist Data**
   Use a database or file to save and load customer data.

This chapter demonstrated how Go's structs, methods, and interfaces work together to enable object-like programming. The practical example of a customer management system showed how to design, implement, and extend a real-world application. In the next chapter, we'll explore Go's concurrency model, focusing on goroutines and channels for building efficient, concurrent applications.

Concurrency in Go

Introduction to Go Routines

Go's concurrency model is one of its standout features. It enables developers to execute multiple tasks simultaneously with minimal effort, thanks to goroutines. Unlike traditional threads, goroutines are lightweight, efficient, and easier to manage, making them ideal for building high-performance, concurrent applications. This chapter will introduce goroutines, explain why they are game-changing, and guide you through building a concurrent web scraper.

What Are Goroutines?

A goroutine is a function that runs concurrently with other functions in the same program. Goroutines are much lighter than traditional threads and can execute thousands (or even millions) of concurrent tasks without significant resource overhead.

Key Characteristics of Goroutines

1. **Lightweight**: Goroutines have a small memory footprint, typically starting at 2 KB of stack space, compared to threads that require several megabytes.

2. **Scalable**: The Go runtime manages goroutines, dynamically growing and shrinking their stack size as needed.

3. **Simple Syntax**: Launching a goroutine is as easy as prefixing a function call with the go keyword.

Why Goroutines Are Game-Changing

1. **Efficient Concurrency**
Goroutines allow you to handle thousands of tasks simultaneously without the overhead of traditional thread management.

2. **Simplicity**
Unlike threads, goroutines abstract away complexities such as manual stack size management and thread creation.

3. **Built-In Communication**
Goroutines use channels to communicate, avoiding common pitfalls like race conditions and deadlocks in multithreaded programming.

Using Goroutines

Launching a Goroutine

The go keyword starts a goroutine:

go

```
package main

import "fmt"

func sayHello() {
    fmt.Println("Hello, World!")
}

func main() {
    go sayHello() // Launch goroutine
    fmt.Println("Main function finished")
}
```

Output (order may vary due to concurrency):

bash

Main function finished

Hello, World!

Concurrency vs. Parallelism

- **Concurrency**: Multiple tasks progress independently, but not necessarily at the same time.

- **Parallelism**: Multiple tasks execute simultaneously on different CPU cores. Go focuses on concurrency but achieves parallelism on multi-core processors.

Waiting for Goroutines

Goroutines run asynchronously. To ensure the program waits for them to complete, use synchronization mechanisms like sync.WaitGroup.

Example:

```go


package main


import (

    "fmt"

    "sync"

)


func sayHello(wg *sync.WaitGroup) {
```

```go
    defer wg.Done() // Notify that the goroutine is done
    fmt.Println("Hello from goroutine")
}

func main() {
    var wg sync.WaitGroup

    wg.Add(1) // Add one task to the WaitGroup
    go sayHello(&wg)

    wg.Wait() // Wait for all tasks to complete
    fmt.Println("All goroutines finished")
}
```

Building a Concurrent Web Scraper

Let's create a web scraper that downloads the HTML content of multiple URLs concurrently using goroutines.

Step 1: Define the Problem

The scraper will:

1. Accept a list of URLs.

2. Fetch each URL's HTML content concurrently.

3. Display the status of each URL.

Step 2: Plan the Solution

1. Use goroutines to fetch URLs concurrently.

2. Employ sync.WaitGroup to ensure all goroutines complete.

3. Add error handling for invalid URLs or network issues.

Step 3: Implement the Code

Here's the full implementation:

go

```go
package main

import (
	"fmt"
	"io/ioutil"
	"net/http"
	"sync"
)
```

```go
func fetchURL(wg *sync.WaitGroup, url string) {
	defer wg.Done() // Notify that the goroutine is done

	// Fetch the URL
	resp, err := http.Get(url)
	if err != nil {
		fmt.Printf("Failed to fetch %s: %v\n", url, err)
		return
	}
	defer resp.Body.Close()

	// Read the response body
	body, err := ioutil.ReadAll(resp.Body)
	if err != nil {
		fmt.Printf("Failed to read response from %s: %v\n", url, err)
		return
	}

	// Print the status and a snippet of the body
```

```go
	fmt.Printf("Fetched %s: Status %d, Snippet: %s...\n", url, resp.StatusCode, string(body[:100]))
}

func main() {
	// List of URLs to scrape
	urls := []string{
		"https://www.example.com",
		"https://www.google.com",
		"https://www.golang.org",
	}

	var wg sync.WaitGroup

	// Launch a goroutine for each URL
	for _, url := range urls {
		wg.Add(1)
		go fetchURL(&wg, url)
	}

	// Wait for all goroutines to finish
	wg.Wait()
```

```
        fmt.Println("All URLs have been fetched")

}
```

Step 4: Run the Program

1. **Save the Code**
   Save the program as web_scraper.go.

2. **Run the Program**

bash

```
go run web_scraper.go
```

3. **Expected Output**

php

```
Fetched https://www.example.com: Status 200,
Snippet: <!doctype html> <html> <head>
<title>Example...

Fetched https://www.google.com: Status 200,
Snippet: <!doctype html> <html itemscope
itemtype="http...

Fetched https://www.golang.org: Status 200, Snippet:
<!DOCTYPE html> <html lang="en"> <head> <meta...

All URLs have been fetched
```

Step 5: Understanding the Code

1. **Goroutines for Fetching**
   Each URL is fetched in its own goroutine using the go keyword.

2. **WaitGroup for Synchronization**
   The sync.WaitGroup ensures the program waits for all goroutines to complete before exiting.

3. **Error Handling**
   Errors are logged without halting the program.

Step 6: Extending the Scraper

1. **Save Content to Files**
   Save the HTML content of each URL to a file:

go

```
filename := fmt.Sprintf("%s.html",
strings.ReplaceAll(url, "https://", ""))

ioutil.WriteFile(filename, body, 0644)
```

2. **Concurrent Rate Limiting**
   Use a channel as a semaphore to limit the number of concurrent goroutines.

3. **Timeout Handling**
   Set a timeout for HTTP requests using a http.Client:

go

```
client := &http.Client{Timeout: 10 * time.Second}

resp, err := client.Get(url)
```

Advantages of Goroutines

1. **High Concurrency**
   A single Go program can manage thousands of
   goroutines, far exceeding the capabilities of
   traditional threads.

2. **Ease of Use**
   Goroutines abstract away complexities like
   thread creation, stack size, and context
   switching.

3. **Scalable Design**
   Applications built with goroutines can scale
   effectively across multiple cores.

This chapter introduced goroutines, their role in Go's
concurrency model, and their advantages over
traditional threading. By building a concurrent web
scraper, you gained hands-on experience with
goroutines, synchronization using sync.WaitGroup,
and error handling in a concurrent environment. In the
next chapter, we'll dive deeper into channels and
synchronization to enhance our understanding of
concurrent programming.

Channels and Synchronization in Go

Goroutines enable efficient concurrency, but they need a way to communicate safely. Go provides channels for this purpose. Channels allow goroutines to send and receive data safely and effectively, enabling synchronization and coordination. In this chapter, you'll learn about channels, how they facilitate communication between goroutines, and how to implement a real-time notification system using them.

Understanding Channels

A **channel** is a conduit through which goroutines can communicate. One goroutine can send data into a channel, and another can receive it.

Defining a Channel

Channels are defined using the chan keyword:

```go
var ch chan int // A channel that transmits integers
```

Creating a Channel

Use the make function to create a channel:

go

ch := make(chan int)

Sending and Receiving Data

- **Send data into a channel:**

go

ch <- 42 // Send the value 42 into the channel

- **Receive data from a channel:**

go

value := <-ch // Receive a value from the channel

Unbuffered vs. Buffered Channels

1. **Unbuffered Channels**
   - Block until both sender and receiver are ready.
   - Useful for synchronization between goroutines.

Example:

```go

ch := make(chan int)


go func() {
    ch <- 42 // Send data
}()


value := <-ch // Receive data
fmt.Println(value) // Outputs: 42
```

2. **Buffered Channels**

- ○ Have a fixed capacity to store data.
- ○ Send operations block only if the buffer is full; receive operations block if the buffer is empty.

Example:

```go


ch := make(chan int, 2) // Create a buffered channel with capacity 2


ch <- 42
```

```go
ch <- 43
```

```go
fmt.Println(<-ch) // Outputs: 42
fmt.Println(<-ch) // Outputs: 43
```

Closing Channels

Closing a channel signals that no more data will be sent. Receivers can detect this with a special value.

- **Closing a Channel:**

```go
close(ch)
```

- **Receiving from a Closed Channel:**

```go
value, ok := <-ch
if !ok {
    fmt.Println("Channel closed")
}
```

Select Statement

The select statement allows a goroutine to wait on multiple channel operations.

Example:

go

ch1 := make(chan int)

ch2 := make(chan string)


```
go func() { ch1 <- 42 }()
go func() { ch2 <- "hello" }()


select {
case msg1 := <-ch1:
    fmt.Println("Received from ch1:", msg1)
case msg2 := <-ch2:
    fmt.Println("Received from ch2:", msg2)
default:
    fmt.Println("No data received")
}
```

Example: Implementing a Real-Time Notification System

Let's use goroutines and channels to build a real-time notification system. The system will:

1. Accept notification messages.

2. Deliver notifications to subscribers in real time.

3. Use channels to handle message communication.

Step 1: Define the Problem

The notification system will:

1. Have a broadcaster that sends notifications.

2. Allow multiple subscribers to receive notifications.

3. Support concurrent delivery using goroutines.

Step 2: Plan the Solution

1. Use a **channel** for broadcasting messages.

2. Launch a **broadcaster goroutine** to send notifications to all subscribers.

3. Use a **slice of channels** to represent subscribers.

Step 3: Implement the Code

Here's the full implementation:

go

```go
package main

import (
        "fmt"
        "sync"
        "time"
)

// Broadcaster manages notification broadcasting
type Broadcaster struct {
        subscribers []chan string
        mu          sync.Mutex
}

// NewBroadcaster initializes a new Broadcaster
func NewBroadcaster() *Broadcaster {
        return &Broadcaster{
                subscribers: []chan string{},
```

```go
        }
}

// Subscribe adds a new subscriber and returns the
subscriber's channel
func (b *Broadcaster) Subscribe() chan string {
        b.mu.Lock()
        defer b.mu.Unlock()

        ch := make(chan string, 1) // Buffered channel
for subscriber
        b.subscribers = append(b.subscribers, ch)
        return ch
}

// Unsubscribe removes a subscriber's channel
func (b *Broadcaster) Unsubscribe(ch chan string) {
        b.mu.Lock()
        defer b.mu.Unlock()

        for i, subscriber := range b.subscribers {
                if subscriber == ch {
```

```go
			b.subscribers =
append(b.subscribers[:i], b.subscribers[i+1:]...)
				close(ch) // Close the channel
				break
			}
		}
	}
}


// Broadcast sends a message to all subscribers
func (b *Broadcaster) Broadcast(message string) {
	b.mu.Lock()
	defer b.mu.Unlock()

	for _, subscriber := range b.subscribers {
		subscriber <- message
	}
}


func main() {
	broadcaster := NewBroadcaster()

	// Create subscribers
```

```go
	subscriber1 := broadcaster.Subscribe()

	subscriber2 := broadcaster.Subscribe()


	// Start listening for messages in separate
goroutines
	go func() {
		for msg := range subscriber1 {
			fmt.Println("Subscriber 1
received:", msg)
		}
	}()


	go func() {
		for msg := range subscriber2 {
			fmt.Println("Subscriber 2
received:", msg)
		}
	}()


	// Broadcast messages
	go func() {
		messages := []string{"Hello, World!", "Go
is awesome!", "Real-time notifications!"}
```

```go
        for _, msg := range messages {
                fmt.Println("Broadcasting:", msg)
                broadcaster.Broadcast(msg)
                time.Sleep(1 * time.Second)
        }

        // Close all channels after broadcasting
        broadcaster.Unsubscribe(subscriber1)
        broadcaster.Unsubscribe(subscriber2)
    }()

    // Allow time for all messages to be processed
    time.Sleep(5 * time.Second)
}
```

Step 4: Understanding the Code

1. **Broadcaster Struct**
   Manages subscribers and broadcasts messages to them via channels.

2. **Synchronization**
   A sync.Mutex ensures safe access to the shared subscribers slice.

3. **Buffered Channels**
   Buffered channels prevent blocking when sending messages.

4. **Goroutines for Subscribers**
   Each subscriber listens for messages in its own goroutine.

Step 5: Run the Program

1. **Save the Code**
   Save the program as notification_system.go.

2. **Run the Program**

bash

```
go run notification_system.go
```

3. **Expected Output**

yaml

```
Broadcasting: Hello, World!

Subscriber 1 received: Hello, World!

Subscriber 2 received: Hello, World!

Broadcasting: Go is awesome!
```

Subscriber 1 received: Go is awesome!

Subscriber 2 received: Go is awesome!

Broadcasting: Real-time notifications!

Subscriber 1 received: Real-time notifications!

Subscriber 2 received: Real-time notifications!

Extending the Notification System

1. **Dynamic Subscriptions**
   Add functionality to subscribe and unsubscribe
   dynamically while broadcasting is active.

2. **Error Handling**
   Handle errors if a subscriber fails to process a
   message.

3. **Persistent Storage**
   Store messages in a database for retrieval in
   case of delivery failures.

Advantages of Channels in Go

1. **Safe Communication**
   Channels eliminate the need for locks when
   exchanging data between goroutines.

2. **Built-In Synchronization**
   Unbuffered channels provide natural synchronization between sender and receiver.

3. **Scalable Design**
   Channels support building scalable, concurrent systems by simplifying communication patterns.

This chapter introduced Go's channels and their role in facilitating communication between goroutines. Through the real-time notification system example, you saw how to use channels for broadcasting, synchronizing, and managing concurrent tasks. In the next chapter, we'll explore advanced concurrency patterns and how to handle more complex communication using select and other tools.

Select Statements and Advanced Concurrency in Go

Concurrency in Go is a powerful tool for building efficient and scalable applications. As applications grow, managing multiple channel operations becomes a common requirement. Go's select statement provides an elegant way to handle this complexity, enabling goroutines to wait on multiple communication operations simultaneously. In this chapter, we'll explore advanced concurrency patterns using select and build a stock price monitoring service as a practical example.

Understanding the select Statement

The select statement in Go is used to handle multiple channel operations. It blocks until one of the channels is ready for communication.

Basic Syntax

go

```
select {
case val := <-ch1:
    fmt.Println("Received from ch1:", val)
case ch2 <- 42:
    fmt.Println("Sent to ch2")
default:
    fmt.Println("No channel operation available")
}
```

Key Features

1. **Blocking Behavior**: select blocks until at least one channel operation can proceed.

2. **Non-Deterministic Selection**: If multiple channels are ready, one is chosen randomly.

3. **Default Case**: Executes immediately if no channels are ready, making select non-blocking.

Advanced Concurrency with select

Timeouts with select

Timeouts prevent goroutines from blocking indefinitely.

Example:

```
go
```

```go
ch := make(chan int)


select {
case val := <-ch:
    fmt.Println("Received:", val)
case <-time.After(2 * time.Second):
    fmt.Println("Timeout occurred")
}
```

Channel Fan-In

Multiple goroutines send data to a single channel, consolidating results.

Example:

```go
```

```go
func producer(ch chan int, id int) {
    for i := 0; i < 3; i++ {
        ch <- id*10 + i
    }
}


func main() {
```

```go
    ch := make(chan int)

    go producer(ch, 1)

    go producer(ch, 2)


    for i := 0; i < 6; i++ {

        fmt.Println(<-ch)

    }

}
```

Channel Fan-Out

A single channel distributes work to multiple worker goroutines.

Example:

```go
go


func worker(ch chan int, id int) {

    for task := range ch {

        fmt.Printf("Worker %d processing task %d\n", id, task)

    }

}


func main() {

    ch := make(chan int)
```

```
for i := 1; i <= 3; i++ {

    go worker(ch, i)

}


for i := 0; i < 10; i++ {

    ch <- i

}

close(ch)

}
```

Example: Building a Stock Price Monitoring Service

Let's apply advanced concurrency to build a service that monitors stock prices from multiple sources and detects significant price changes.

Step 1: Define the Problem

The stock price monitoring service will:

1. Fetch stock prices concurrently from multiple sources.

2. Consolidate price updates into a single channel.

3. Trigger alerts for significant price changes.

Step 2: Plan the Solution

1. **Source Goroutines**
   Each source fetches stock prices and sends updates to a shared channel.

2. **Aggregator Goroutine**
   Consolidates data from all sources and processes updates.

3. **Alert Mechanism**
   Detects significant price changes and triggers notifications.

Step 3: Implement the Code

Here's the full implementation:

go

```go
package main

import (
    "fmt"
    "math/rand"
    "sync"
    "time"
```

```go
)

// PriceUpdate represents a stock price update
type PriceUpdate struct {
        Stock string
        Price float64
}

// FetchPrices simulates fetching stock prices from a
source
func FetchPrices(stock string, ch chan PriceUpdate,
wg *sync.WaitGroup) {
        defer wg.Done()

        for i := 0; i < 5; i++ {
                // Simulate fetching price
                price := rand.Float64() * 100
                ch <- PriceUpdate{Stock: stock, Price:
price}

                // Random delay to simulate real-world
updates
```

```go
        time.Sleep(time.Duration(rand.Intn(1000)) *
time.Millisecond)
        }
}


// MonitorPrices processes price updates and triggers
alerts
func MonitorPrices(ch chan PriceUpdate, stop chan
bool) {
        previousPrices := make(map[string]float64)

        for {
                select {
                case update := <-ch:
                        fmt.Printf("Received update: %s -
$%.2f\n", update.Stock, update.Price)


                        // Check for significant price
changes
                        if prev, ok :=
previousPrices[update.Stock]; ok {
                                change := (update.Price -
prev) / prev * 100
```

```go
                    if change > 10 || change <
-10 {
                            fmt.Printf("ALERT:
Significant price change for %s: %.2f%%\n",
update.Stock, change)
                    }
                }


                previousPrices[update.Stock] =
update.Price


            case <-stop:
                fmt.Println("Stopping
monitoring...")
                return
            }
        }
}


func main() {
    rand.Seed(time.Now().UnixNano())

    // Channel for price updates
    priceChannel := make(chan PriceUpdate, 10)
```

```go
// Stop channel to terminate monitoring
stopChannel := make(chan bool)

// List of stocks to monitor
stocks := []string{"AAPL", "GOOG", "AMZN"}

// WaitGroup to synchronize source goroutines
var wg sync.WaitGroup

// Launch source goroutines
for _, stock := range stocks {
        wg.Add(1)
        go FetchPrices(stock, priceChannel, &wg)
}

// Launch monitor goroutine
go MonitorPrices(priceChannel, stopChannel)

// Wait for all sources to finish
wg.Wait()
```

```
// Stop the monitor goroutine

stopChannel <- true


fmt.Println("All done!")
}
```

Step 4: Understanding the Code

1. **Source Goroutines**
   Each source simulates fetching stock prices
   and sends updates to the shared channel.

2. **Monitor Goroutine**

   o   Consolidates updates from all sources
       using a select statement.

   o   Tracks price changes in a map and
       detects significant changes.

3. **Stop Channel**
   A dedicated stop channel gracefully stops the
   monitor goroutine.

Step 5: Run the Program

1. **Save the Code**
   Save the program as stock_monitor.go.

2. **Run the Program**

bash

```
go run stock_monitor.go
```

3. **Expected Output**

yaml

```
Received update: AAPL - $45.67
Received update: GOOG - $76.45
Received update: AMZN - $54.23
ALERT: Significant price change for AAPL: 15.34%
ALERT: Significant price change for GOOG: -12.67%
...
Stopping monitoring...
All done!
```

Step 6: Extending the Service

1. **Add More Sources**
   Integrate real stock price APIs using the net/http package.

2. **Enhanced Alerts**
    Add thresholds for different stocks or send
    alerts via email/SMS.

3. **Web Dashboard**
    Create a live dashboard using the net/http and
    html/template packages to display price
    updates.

Advantages of select and Advanced Concurrency

1. **Efficient Coordination**
    The select statement enables smooth handling
    of multiple channel operations.

2. **Scalable Design**
    Advanced concurrency patterns like fan-in and
    fan-out support high-performance systems.

3. **Graceful Termination**
    Combining channels and select ensures clean
    and controlled shutdowns of goroutines.

This chapter introduced advanced concurrency
techniques in Go, focusing on the select statement for
handling multiple channel operations. Through the
stock price monitoring service example, you learned
how to consolidate data, detect changes, and manage
goroutines effectively.

Building Applications

Working with Files and Data in Go

Handling files is a fundamental skill in programming, and Go provides a rich set of tools in its os, io, and bufio packages for working with files and data. This chapter explores how to read from and write to files in Go, with a practical example of building a configuration file manager.

Reading from Files

Reading files in Go can be done using various techniques depending on the use case.

Reading the Entire File

The os and io/ioutil packages can be used to read an entire file into memory.

Example:

```go


package main


import (
```

```go
    "fmt"

    "io/ioutil"

    "log"
)


func main() {

    data, err := ioutil.ReadFile("config.txt")

    if err != nil {

        log.Fatalf("Failed to read file: %s", err)

    }


    fmt.Println("File Contents:")

    fmt.Println(string(data))
}
```

Reading Files Line by Line

For large files, reading line by line using bufio.Scanner is more efficient.

Example:

go

package main

```go
import (
        "bufio"
        "fmt"
        "os"
)

func main() {
        file, err := os.Open("config.txt")
        if err != nil {
                fmt.Println("Error opening file:", err)
                return
        }
        defer file.Close()

        scanner := bufio.NewScanner(file)
        for scanner.Scan() {
                fmt.Println(scanner.Text())
        }

        if err := scanner.Err(); err != nil {
                fmt.Println("Error reading file:", err)
        }
```

```
}
```

Writing to Files

Go provides straightforward ways to create and write to files.

Writing Data to a New File

The os.Create function creates a new file and writes data to it.

Example:

```go
package main

import (
        "fmt"
        "os"
)

func main() {
        file, err := os.Create("output.txt")
        if err != nil {
                fmt.Println("Error creating file:", err)
```

```go
		return
	}
	defer file.Close()

	_, err = file.WriteString("Hello, Go!\n")
	if err != nil {
		fmt.Println("Error writing to file:", err)
		return
	}

	fmt.Println("Data written successfully!")
}
```

Appending to an Existing File

The os.OpenFile function allows appending data to an existing file.

Example:

go

```go
package main

import (
	"fmt"
```

```go
	"os"
)


func main() {
	file, err := os.OpenFile("output.txt",
os.O_APPEND|os.O_WRONLY, 0644)
	if err != nil {
		fmt.Println("Error opening file:", err)
		return
	}
	defer file.Close()


	_, err = file.WriteString("Appended line\n")
	if err != nil {
		fmt.Println("Error appending to file:", err)
		return
	}


	fmt.Println("Data appended successfully!")
}
```

Working with JSON Configuration Files

Go's encoding/json package simplifies reading and writing JSON files, which are commonly used for configuration.

Reading a JSON File

Example config.json:

json

```json
{

    "app_name": "FileManager",

    "port": 8080,

    "debug": true

}
```

Reading and parsing:

go

```go
package main

import (
        "encoding/json"
        "fmt"
```

```go
	"io/ioutil"
	"log"
)


type Config struct {
	AppName string `json:"app_name"`
	Port    int    `json:"port"`
	Debug   bool   `json:"debug"`
}


func main() {
	data, err := ioutil.ReadFile("config.json")
	if err != nil {
		log.Fatalf("Failed to read file: %s", err)
	}


	var config Config
	err = json.Unmarshal(data, &config)
	if err != nil {
		log.Fatalf("Failed to parse JSON: %s", err)
	}
```

```go
        fmt.Printf("Config: %+v\n", config)
}
```

Writing to a JSON File

```go
package main

import (
        "encoding/json"
        "fmt"
        "os"
)

type Config struct {
        AppName string `json:"app_name"`
        Port    int    `json:"port"`
        Debug   bool   `json:"debug"`
}

func main() {
        config := Config{
```

```go
        AppName: "FileManager",
        Port:    8080,
        Debug:   true,
    }

    file, err := os.Create("new_config.json")
    if err != nil {
        fmt.Println("Error creating file:", err)
        return
    }
    defer file.Close()

    encoder := json.NewEncoder(file)
    err = encoder.Encode(config)
    if err != nil {
        fmt.Println("Error writing JSON to file:",
err)
        return
    }

    fmt.Println("Configuration saved to file.")
}
```

Example: Creating a Configuration File Manager

Now let's build a practical configuration file manager that can:

1. Load configuration from a file.

2. Update specific configuration values.

3. Save the updated configuration back to the file.

Step 1: Define the Problem

The manager will:

1. Support loading a JSON configuration file.

2. Allow the user to modify configuration values interactively.

3. Save the modified configuration to a file.

Step 2: Plan the Solution

1. Define a Config struct to map the configuration fields.

2. Create functions to load, update, and save the configuration.

3. Use a simple menu interface for interaction.

Step 3: Implement the Code

Here's the full implementation:

go

```go
package main

import (
        "encoding/json"
        "fmt"
        "io/ioutil"
        "os"
)

type Config struct {
        AppName string `json:"app_name"`
        Port    int    `json:"port"`
        Debug   bool   `json:"debug"`
}

func loadConfig(filename string) (*Config, error) {
        data, err := ioutil.ReadFile(filename)
```

```go
	if err != nil {
		return nil, fmt.Errorf("failed to read file: %w", err)
	}

	var config Config
	err = json.Unmarshal(data, &config)
	if err != nil {
		return nil, fmt.Errorf("failed to parse JSON: %w", err)
	}

	return &config, nil
}

func saveConfig(filename string, config *Config) error {
	file, err := os.Create(filename)
	if err != nil {
		return fmt.Errorf("failed to create file: %w", err)
	}
	defer file.Close()
```

```go
        encoder := json.NewEncoder(file)

        err = encoder.Encode(config)

        if err != nil {

                return fmt.Errorf("failed to write JSON: %w", err)

        }


        return nil

}


func main() {

        filename := "config.json"


        // Load configuration

        config, err := loadConfig(filename)

        if err != nil {

                fmt.Println("Error:", err)

                return

        }


        fmt.Println("Current Configuration:")
```

```go
	fmt.Printf("App Name: %s\n", config.AppName)
	fmt.Printf("Port: %d\n", config.Port)
	fmt.Printf("Debug Mode: %v\n", config.Debug)

	// Update configuration interactively
	fmt.Println("\nUpdate Configuration:")
	fmt.Print("Enter new app name: ")
	fmt.Scanln(&config.AppName)

	fmt.Print("Enter new port: ")
	fmt.Scanln(&config.Port)

	fmt.Print("Enable debug mode (true/false): ")
	fmt.Scanln(&config.Debug)

	// Save updated configuration
	err = saveConfig(filename, config)
	if err != nil {
		fmt.Println("Error saving configuration:", err)
		return
	}
```

```go
        fmt.Println("Configuration updated
successfully!")
}
```

Step 4: Run the Program

1. Prepare a config.json File

json

```json
{
    "app_name": "FileManager",
    "port": 8080,
    "debug": true
}
```

2. Run the Program

bash

```bash
go run config_manager.go
```

3. Expected Output

yaml

Current Configuration:

App Name: FileManager

Port: 8080

Debug Mode: true

Update Configuration:

Enter new app name: MyApp

Enter new port: 9090

Enable debug mode (true/false): false

Configuration updated successfully!

4. **Updated config.json**

json


```json
{

  "app_name": "MyApp",

  "port": 9090,

  "debug": false

}
```

Extending the Configuration Manager

1. **Validation**
   Add validation for user inputs to ensure data integrity (e.g., port must be within 1–65535).

2. **Multiple File Support**
   Allow managing multiple configuration files by passing the filename as a command-line argument.

3. **Command-Line Flags**
   Use flag package to set configuration values directly from the command line.

4. **Encrypted Configuration**
   Add support for encrypting sensitive configuration data using Go's crypto package.

This chapter covered the fundamentals of working with files and data in Go, including reading and writing files and handling JSON configurations. Through the configuration file manager example, you saw how to load, update, and save configurations interactively. In the next chapter, we'll dive into working with databases in Go to persist and query structured data.

Working with Databases in Go

Databases are a crucial part of most applications, allowing persistent storage and retrieval of structured data. Go provides robust tools for working with databases through the database/sql package and third-party libraries. In this chapter, we'll explore using SQL databases with Go, culminating in the development of a task management app with persistent storage.

Understanding database/sql

The database/sql package in Go is a standard library for interacting with SQL databases. It provides a generic interface for database operations and works with various SQL drivers like sqlite3, mysql, and postgres.

Installing a Database Driver

Choose a driver based on your database. For this example, we'll use SQLite for simplicity.

Install the SQLite driver:

bash

```
go get modernc.org/sqlite
```

Import the driver in your program:

```go
```

```
import _ "modernc.org/sqlite"
```

Connecting to a Database

To interact with a database, create a connection using sql.Open.

Example:

```go
```

```go
package main

import (
        "database/sql"
        "fmt"
        "log"
        _ "modernc.org/sqlite"
)
```

```go
func main() {

        db, err := sql.Open("sqlite", "tasks.db")

        if err != nil {

                log.Fatalf("Failed to connect to
database: %v", err)

        }

        defer db.Close()


        fmt.Println("Database connection established")

}
```

- **sql.Open**: Opens a connection to the database.
- **Driver Name**: Matches the driver you're using (sqlite for SQLite, mysql for MySQL, etc.).
- **Data Source Name (DSN)**: Specifies the database file or connection string.

Creating Tables

Define the structure of your data using SQL CREATE TABLE statements.

Example:

go

```go
_, err = db.Exec(`
CREATE TABLE IF NOT EXISTS tasks (
    id INTEGER PRIMARY KEY AUTOINCREMENT,
    title TEXT NOT NULL,
    completed BOOLEAN NOT NULL
)`)
if err != nil {
    log.Fatalf("Failed to create table: %v", err)
}
fmt.Println("Table created or already exists")
```

CRUD Operations in Go

CRUD stands for Create, Read, Update, Delete. Let's explore each operation.

Create (Insert Data)

Use db.Exec to execute SQL INSERT statements.

Example:

go

```go
_, err = db.Exec("INSERT INTO tasks (title, completed) VALUES (?, ?)", "Learn Go", false)
if err != nil {
```

```go
        log.Fatalf("Failed to insert task: %v", err)
}
fmt.Println("Task added successfully")
```

Read (Query Data)

Use db.Query or db.QueryRow to fetch data from the database.

Example:

go

```go
rows, err := db.Query("SELECT id, title, completed FROM tasks")
if err != nil {
        log.Fatalf("Failed to query tasks: %v", err)
}
defer rows.Close()

for rows.Next() {
        var id int
        var title string
        var completed bool

        err = rows.Scan(&id, &title, &completed)
        if err != nil {
```

```
        log.Fatalf("Failed to read row: %v", err)

    }
```

```
    fmt.Printf("Task %d: %s (Completed: %v)\n",
id, title, completed)

}
```

Update (Modify Data)

Use db.Exec with an UPDATE statement to modify
records.

Example:

```go
_, err = db.Exec("UPDATE tasks SET completed = ?
WHERE id = ?", true, 1)

if err != nil {

        log.Fatalf("Failed to update task: %v", err)

}

fmt.Println("Task updated successfully")
```

Delete (Remove Data)

Use db.Exec with a DELETE statement to delete
records.

Example:

```go
```

```
_, err = db.Exec("DELETE FROM tasks WHERE id =
?", 1)

if err != nil {

        log.Fatalf("Failed to delete task: %v", err)

}

fmt.Println("Task deleted successfully")
```

Example: Designing a Task Management App

Let's build a task management app with persistent storage using SQLite.

Step 1: Define the Problem

The app will:

1. Store tasks in a SQLite database.

2. Allow users to:

    o Add new tasks.

    o List all tasks.

    o Mark tasks as completed.

    o Delete tasks.

Step 2: Plan the Solution

1. Use SQLite for persistent storage.

2. Create a tasks table to store task information.

3. Implement CLI commands for interacting with tasks.

Step 3: Implement the Code

Here's the complete implementation:

go

```go
package main

import (
        "database/sql"
        "fmt"
        "log"
        "os"
        "strconv"

        _ "modernc.org/sqlite"
)
```

```go
func main() {
	// Connect to the database
	db, err := sql.Open("sqlite", "tasks.db")
	if err != nil {
		log.Fatalf("Failed to connect to database: %v", err)
	}
	defer db.Close()

	// Create the tasks table
	_, err = db.Exec(`
	CREATE TABLE IF NOT EXISTS tasks (
		id INTEGER PRIMARY KEY AUTOINCREMENT,
		title TEXT NOT NULL,
		completed BOOLEAN NOT NULL
	)`)
	if err != nil {
		log.Fatalf("Failed to create table: %v", err)
	}

	// Parse CLI arguments
```

```go
    if len(os.Args) < 2 {
        fmt.Println("Usage: go run main.go
[add|list|complete|delete] [arguments...]")
        return
    }

    switch os.Args[1] {
    case "add":
        addTask(db, os.Args[2:])
    case "list":
        listTasks(db)
    case "complete":
        completeTask(db, os.Args[2:])
    case "delete":
        deleteTask(db, os.Args[2:])
    default:
        fmt.Println("Invalid command")
    }
}

func addTask(db *sql.DB, args []string) {
    if len(args) < 1 {
```

```go
		fmt.Println("Usage: go run main.go add
[task_title]")
		return
	}
	title := args[0]

	_, err := db.Exec("INSERT INTO tasks (title,
completed) VALUES (?, ?)", title, false)
	if err != nil {
		log.Fatalf("Failed to add task: %v", err)
	}
	fmt.Println("Task added successfully")
}


func listTasks(db *sql.DB) {
	rows, err := db.Query("SELECT id, title,
completed FROM tasks")
	if err != nil {
		log.Fatalf("Failed to query tasks: %v",
err)
	}
	defer rows.Close()

	fmt.Println("Tasks:")
```

```go
	for rows.Next() {
		var id int
		var title string
		var completed bool
		err = rows.Scan(&id, &title, &completed)
		if err != nil {
			log.Fatalf("Failed to read row: %v", err)
		}
		status := "Pending"
		if completed {
			status = "Completed"
		}
		fmt.Printf("%d: %s [%s]\n", id, title, status)
	}
}


func completeTask(db *sql.DB, args []string) {
	if len(args) < 1 {
		fmt.Println("Usage: go run main.go complete [task_id]")
		return
```

```go
	}
	id, err := strconv.Atoi(args[0])
	if err != nil {
		log.Fatalf("Invalid task ID: %v", err)
	}
	_, err = db.Exec("UPDATE tasks SET
completed = ? WHERE id = ?", true, id)
	if err != nil {
		log.Fatalf("Failed to complete task: %v",
err)
	}
	fmt.Println("Task marked as completed")
}


func deleteTask(db *sql.DB, args []string) {
	if len(args) < 1 {
		fmt.Println("Usage: go run main.go
delete [task_id]")
		return
	}
	id, err := strconv.Atoi(args[0])
	if err != nil {
		log.Fatalf("Invalid task ID: %v", err)
```

```go
    }

    _, err = db.Exec("DELETE FROM tasks
WHERE id = ?", id)

    if err != nil {

        log.Fatalf("Failed to delete task: %v",
err)

    }

    fmt.Println("Task deleted successfully")

}
```

Step 4: Run the Program

1. **Build the Application**
   Save the program as task_manager.go.

2. **Run Commands**

   o Add a task:

bash

go run task_manager.go add "Learn Go"

   o List tasks:

bash

go run task_manager.go list

      o   Complete a task:

bash

go run task_manager.go complete 1

      o   Delete a task:

bash

go run task_manager.go delete 1

Step 5: Expected Output

1. Add a task:

arduino

Task added successfully

2. List tasks:

makefile

Tasks:

1: Learn Go [Pending]

3. Complete a task:

arduino

Task marked as completed

    4. Delete a task:

arduino

Task deleted successfully

Extending the App

1. **Search Tasks**
    Add a command to search tasks by title.

2. **Due Dates**
    Include a due_date field in the tasks table.

3. **Web Interface**
    Build a web interface using a framework like
    Gin for managing tasks.

4. **Notifications**
    Add a feature to send reminders for pending
    tasks.

This chapter covered the essentials of working with
SQL databases in Go using the database/sql
package. By building a task management app, you

learned how to perform CRUD operations and handle user input via a CLI. In the next chapter, we'll explore building REST APIs to make applications accessible over the web.

Building REST APIs in Go

REST APIs are essential for enabling communication between client applications and backend servers. Go's standard library provides the net/http package, which makes building RESTful services straightforward and efficient. This chapter explores how to create a REST API in Go and demonstrates it by building a simple product inventory management system.

Understanding REST and HTTP in Go

1. **What is REST?**
   REST (Representational State Transfer) is an architectural style for APIs, emphasizing:

   - **Statelessness**: Each request contains all information needed for processing.

   - **HTTP Methods**: Use methods like GET, POST, PUT, and DELETE for operations.

   - **Resource URLs**: Resources are identified via meaningful URLs.

2. **Go's HTTP Package**
   The net/http package provides essential tools for building HTTP servers and handling requests.

Setting Up a Basic HTTP Server

Example: A Simple HTTP Server

go

```go
package main

import (
        "fmt"
        "net/http"
)

func handler(w http.ResponseWriter, r *http.Request) {
        fmt.Fprintf(w, "Hello, World!")
}

func main() {
```

```
    http.HandleFunc("/", handler)

    fmt.Println("Server is running on
http://localhost:8080")

    http.ListenAndServe(":8080", nil)
}
```

- **http.HandleFunc**: Maps a URL pattern to a handler function.

- **http.ListenAndServe**: Starts the HTTP server on a specified port.

Building a Product Inventory REST API

Let's create a REST API to manage a product inventory, implementing CRUD operations for products.

Step 1: Define the Problem

The API will:

1. Add new products to the inventory.

2. List all products.

3. Update product details.

4. Delete products.

Step 2: Plan the Solution

1. Define a Product struct to represent inventory items.

2. Use an in-memory slice as the data store for simplicity.

3. Implement HTTP handlers for each API endpoint.

Step 3: Implement the Code

Here's the complete implementation:

go

```go
package main

import (
	"encoding/json"
	"fmt"
	"net/http"
	"strconv"
	"sync"
)

// Product represents an inventory item
type Product struct {
```

```go
        ID     int     `json:"id"`
        Name   string  `json:"name"`
        Price  float64 `json:"price"`
        Stock  int     `json:"stock"`
}


// Global variables
var (
        products []Product
        mutex    sync.Mutex
        nextID   = 1
)


func main() {
        http.HandleFunc("/products", handleProducts)
        http.HandleFunc("/products/",
handleProductByID)


        fmt.Println("Server is running on
http://localhost:8080")
        http.ListenAndServe(":8080", nil)
}
```

```go
// Handle requests for /products
func handleProducts(w http.ResponseWriter, r *http.Request) {

    switch r.Method {

    case http.MethodGet:

        listProducts(w)

    case http.MethodPost:

        addProduct(w, r)

    default:

        http.Error(w, "Method not allowed", http.StatusMethodNotAllowed)

    }

}


// Handle requests for /products/{id}
func handleProductByID(w http.ResponseWriter, r *http.Request) {

    id, err := strconv.Atoi(r.URL.Path[len("/products/"):])

    if err != nil {

        http.Error(w, "Invalid product ID", http.StatusBadRequest)

        return

    }
```

```go
        switch r.Method {
        case http.MethodGet:
                getProduct(w, id)
        case http.MethodPut:
                updateProduct(w, r, id)
        case http.MethodDelete:
                deleteProduct(w, id)
        default:
                http.Error(w, "Method not allowed",
http.StatusMethodNotAllowed)
        }
}


// List all products
func listProducts(w http.ResponseWriter) {
        mutex.Lock()
        defer mutex.Unlock()


        w.Header().Set("Content-Type",
"application/json")
        json.NewEncoder(w).Encode(products)
}
```

```go
// Add a new product
func addProduct(w http.ResponseWriter, r *http.Request) {
        var product Product
        err := json.NewDecoder(r.Body).Decode(&product)
        if err != nil {
                http.Error(w, "Invalid request body", http.StatusBadRequest)
                return
        }

        mutex.Lock()
        defer mutex.Unlock()

        product.ID = nextID
        nextID++
        products = append(products, product)

        w.WriteHeader(http.StatusCreated)
        json.NewEncoder(w).Encode(product)
}
```

```go
// Get a product by ID
func getProduct(w http.ResponseWriter, id int) {
        mutex.Lock()
        defer mutex.Unlock()

        for _, product := range products {
                if product.ID == id {
                        w.Header().Set("Content-Type", "application/json")

                        json.NewEncoder(w).Encode(product)
                        return
                }
        }

        http.Error(w, "Product not found", http.StatusNotFound)
}

// Update a product by ID
func updateProduct(w http.ResponseWriter, r *http.Request, id int) {
```

```go
var updatedProduct Product
err := json.NewDecoder(r.Body).Decode(&updatedProduct)
if err != nil {
    http.Error(w, "Invalid request body", http.StatusBadRequest)
    return
}

mutex.Lock()
defer mutex.Unlock()

for i, product := range products {
    if product.ID == id {
        products[i].Name = updatedProduct.Name
        products[i].Price = updatedProduct.Price
        products[i].Stock = updatedProduct.Stock

        w.Header().Set("Content-Type", "application/json")
```

```go
            json.NewEncoder(w).Encode(products[i])
            return
        }
    }

    http.Error(w, "Product not found",
http.StatusNotFound)
}


// Delete a product by ID
func deleteProduct(w http.ResponseWriter, id int) {
        mutex.Lock()
        defer mutex.Unlock()

        for i, product := range products {
                if product.ID == id {
                        products = append(products[:i],
products[i+1:]...)

                        w.WriteHeader(http.StatusNoContent)
                        return
                }
```

```
        }

        http.Error(w, "Product not found",
http.StatusNotFound)
}
```

Step 4: Run the API

1. Save the code as product_api.go.

2. Run the server:

bash

```
go run product_api.go
```

3. Access the API at http://localhost:8080.

Step 5: Test the API

1. **List All Products**

bash

```
curl http://localhost:8080/products
```

2. **Add a Product**

bash

```
curl -X POST -H "Content-Type: application/json" -d
'{"name":"Laptop","price":1200.50,"stock":10}'
http://localhost:8080/products
```

3. Get a Product by ID

bash

```
curl http://localhost:8080/products/1
```

4. Update a Product

bash

```
curl -X PUT -H "Content-Type: application/json" -d
'{"name":"Gaming Laptop","price":1500.00,"stock":5}'
http://localhost:8080/products/1
```

5. Delete a Product

bash

```
curl -X DELETE http://localhost:8080/products/1
```

Extending the API

1. **Pagination**
   Add query parameters for pagination (e.g., /products?page=1&limit=10).

2. **Search**
   Implement search functionality by product name or price range.

3. **Persistent Storage**
   Replace the in-memory store with a database like SQLite or PostgreSQL.

4. **Authentication**
   Secure the API with authentication using tokens (e.g., JWT).

5. **Rate Limiting**
   Prevent abuse by implementing rate limiting.

Advantages of Go for REST APIs

1. **Lightweight**: The net/http package provides a simple yet powerful foundation.

2. **Performance**: Go's compiled nature and efficient concurrency model make it ideal for high-performance APIs.

3. **Extensibility**: Middleware and third-party libraries (e.g., gorilla/mux) enhance functionality.

This chapter demonstrated how to create REST APIs in Go using the net/http package. Through the product inventory example, you learned to implement CRUD operations and handle different HTTP methods.

Building Web Applications in Go

Go is well-suited for web development, offering a robust standard library (net/http) and several powerful web frameworks. Whether you're creating simple websites or complex platforms, Go provides the tools to make development efficient and scalable. This chapter focuses on using Go templating and web frameworks, culminating in the creation of a basic e-commerce platform.

Understanding Go's Templating System

Go's standard library includes the html/template package for dynamic HTML generation. Templates allow you to separate HTML from your application logic, promoting clean and maintainable code.

Basic Template Usage

1. **Creating a Template**
   Define an HTML template as a string or file.

html

```
{{define "example"}}
```

```html
<html>
<head><title>{{.Title}}</title></head>
<body>
    <h1>{{.Message}}</h1>
</body>
</html>
{{end}}
```

2. **Parsing and Executing the Template**
   Use template.ParseFiles to load templates and
   Execute to render them.

go

```go
package main

import (
    "html/template"
    "net/http"
)

type Page struct {
    Title   string
    Message string
}
```

```go
func handler(w http.ResponseWriter, r *http.Request)
{

    tmpl, _ := template.ParseFiles("example.html")

    data := Page{Title: "Welcome", Message: "Hello,
Go Web!"}

    tmpl.Execute(w, data)

}


func main() {

    http.HandleFunc("/", handler)

    http.ListenAndServe(":8080", nil)

}
```

Go Web Frameworks

While Go's standard library is sufficient for many web applications, frameworks like Gin, Echo, and Fiber streamline development by adding features like routing, middleware, and request validation.

Choosing a Framework

1. **Gin**: Lightweight and fast with excellent middleware support.

2. **Echo**: Simple, scalable, and focuses on high performance.

3. **Fiber**: Inspired by Express.js, it emphasizes ease of use and speed.

For our example, we'll use the Gin framework.

Example: Developing a Basic E-Commerce Platform

Let's create a simple e-commerce platform that:

1. Displays a list of products.

2. Allows users to add products to a cart.

3. Renders pages using Go templates.

Step 1: Define the Problem

The e-commerce platform will:

1. Display products on the homepage.

2. Show a shopping cart page listing selected items.

3. Use an in-memory store for simplicity.

Step 2: Plan the Solution

1. **Products**
   Define a struct to represent products with fields like ID, name, price, and description.

2. **Cart**
   Use a slice to store cart items.

3. **Pages**
   Create HTML templates for the homepage and cart.

4. **Routes**
   Implement routes for:

   - /: Displaying products.

   - /cart: Viewing the cart.

   - /add-to-cart/:id: Adding products to the cart.

Step 3: Implement the Code

Directory Structure

css

```
ecommerce/
├── main.go
├── templates/
|   ├── index.html
|   └── cart.html
```

Code Implementation

1. main.go: The Application Logic

go

```go
package main

import (
	"fmt"
	"html/template"
	"net/http"
	"strconv"

	"github.com/gin-gonic/gin"
)

// Product represents an item in the store
type Product struct {
	ID      int
	Name    string
	Price   float64
```

```go
        Description string
}


// Global variables
var (
        products = []Product{
                {ID: 1, Name: "Laptop", Price: 1200.00,
Description: "High-performance laptop"},
                {ID: 2, Name: "Phone", Price: 800.00,
Description: "Latest smartphone"},
                {ID: 3, Name: "Headphones", Price:
150.00, Description: "Noise-cancelling headphones"},
        }
        cart []Product
)


func main() {
        r := gin.Default()


        // Load templates
        r.LoadHTMLGlob("templates/*")


        // Routes
```

```go
    r.GET("/", showProducts)
    r.GET("/cart", showCart)
    r.GET("/add-to-cart/:id", addToCart)

    // Start server
    r.Run(":8080")
}


// Show the list of products
func showProducts(c *gin.Context) {
    c.HTML(http.StatusOK, "index.html", gin.H{
        "products": products,
    })
}


// Show the shopping cart
func showCart(c *gin.Context) {
    c.HTML(http.StatusOK, "cart.html", gin.H{
        "cart": cart,
    })
}
```

```go
// Add a product to the cart
func addToCart(c *gin.Context) {
    id, err := strconv.Atoi(c.Param("id"))
    if err != nil {
        c.String(http.StatusBadRequest, "Invalid product ID")
        return
    }

    for _, product := range products {
        if product.ID == id {
            cart = append(cart, product)
            c.String(http.StatusOK, "Added to cart: %s", product.Name)
            return
        }
    }

    c.String(http.StatusNotFound, "Product not found")
}
```

---

2. Templates

index.html: The Homepage Template

html

```html
<!DOCTYPE html>
<html lang="en">
<head>
  <meta charset="UTF-8">
  <title>Products</title>
</head>
<body>
  <h1>Products</h1>
  <ul>
    {{range .products}}
    <li>
      <strong>{{.Name}}</strong> - ${{.Price}}
      <p>{{.Description}}</p>
      <a href="/add-to-cart/{{.ID}}">Add to Cart</a>
    </li>
    {{end}}
  </ul>
  <a href="/cart">View Cart</a>
</body>
```

</html>

cart.html: The Cart Template

html

```html
<!DOCTYPE html>
<html lang="en">
<head>
  <meta charset="UTF-8">
  <title>Shopping Cart</title>
</head>
<body>
  <h1>Shopping Cart</h1>
  <ul>
    {{range .cart}}
    <li>
      <strong>{{.Name}}</strong> - ${{.Price}}
      <p>{{.Description}}</p>
    </li>
    {{end}}
  </ul>
  <a href="/">Back to Products</a>
</body>
```

```
</html>
```

Step 4: Run the Application

1. **Install Gin**

bash

```
go get -u github.com/gin-gonic/gin
```

2. **Run the Application**

bash

```
go run main.go
```

3. **Access the Application**

   o Visit http://localhost:8080 to see the
     product list.

   o Click "Add to Cart" to add items to the
     cart.

   o Visit /cart to view selected items.

Step 5: Expected Output

1. **Homepage**

bash

Products

- Laptop: $1200.00 (Add to Cart)

- Phone: $800.00 (Add to Cart)

- Headphones: $150.00 (Add to Cart)

2. **Cart**

bash

Shopping Cart

- Laptop: $1200.00

- Phone: $800.00

Extending the E-Commerce Platform

1. **Persistent Storage**
   Replace the in-memory data store with a database like SQLite or PostgreSQL.

2. **Authentication**
   Implement user accounts and login functionality.

3. **Checkout System**
   Add a payment gateway integration to handle purchases.

4. **Dynamic Pricing**
   Enable discounts and dynamic price updates.

5. **Admin Panel**
   Create an admin interface for adding, updating, and deleting products.

Advantages of Go for Web Applications

1. **Efficiency**: Go's performance and concurrency model handle high-traffic applications effectively.

2. **Lightweight Frameworks**: Minimal overhead makes applications fast and responsive.

3. **Scalability**: Ideal for scaling applications horizontally across multiple servers.

This chapter demonstrated how to build web applications in Go using templates and frameworks. By creating a basic e-commerce platform, you learned to manage routes, render templates, and handle user interactions.

Advanced Topics

Testing and Benchmarking in Go

Testing and benchmarking are vital aspects of software development. They ensure your code is correct, robust, and performant. Go's standard library includes a powerful testing package that simplifies writing unit tests and benchmarking. This chapter explores testing and benchmarking in Go with a practical example: writing unit tests and benchmarks for a calculator module.

Understanding Go's Testing Package

The testing package provides tools for writing tests and benchmarks. Go treats test files with the _test.go suffix as special and runs them using the go test command.

Writing a Test Function

1. Test functions start with Test and take a single *testing.T parameter.

2. Use methods on *testing.T (like t.Errorf or t.Fatal) to indicate failures.

Example:

go

```go
package main

import "testing"

func Add(a, b int) int {
        return a + b
}

func TestAdd(t *testing.T) {
        result := Add(2, 3)
        expected := 5
        if result != expected {
                t.Errorf("Add(2, 3) = %d; want %d", result, expected)
        }
}
```

Running Tests

Run tests using:

bash

```
go test
```

Output:

```arduino
PASS
ok      module-name      0.001s
```

Writing Unit Tests

Let's write tests for a simple calculator module that performs basic arithmetic operations.

Step 1: Implement the Calculator Module

calculator.go:

```go
package calculator

// Add returns the sum of two integers.
func Add(a, b int) int {
    return a + b
}
```

```go
// Subtract returns the difference of two integers.
func Subtract(a, b int) int {
        return a - b
}


// Multiply returns the product of two integers.
func Multiply(a, b int) int {
        return a * b
}


// Divide returns the quotient of two integers.
func Divide(a, b int) (int, error) {
        if b == 0 {
                return 0, fmt.Errorf("cannot divide by zero")
        }
        return a / b, nil
}
```

Step 2: Write Unit Tests

calculator_test.go:

```go
package calculator

import (
	"testing"
)

func TestAdd(t *testing.T) {
	result := Add(2, 3)
	expected := 5
	if result != expected {
		t.Errorf("Add(2, 3) = %d; want %d",
result, expected)
	}
}

func TestSubtract(t *testing.T) {
	result := Subtract(5, 3)
	expected := 2
	if result != expected {
		t.Errorf("Subtract(5, 3) = %d; want %d",
result, expected)
```

```go
		}
}


func TestMultiply(t *testing.T) {
	result := Multiply(4, 5)
	expected := 20
	if result != expected {
		t.Errorf("Multiply(4, 5) = %d; want %d",
result, expected)
	}
}


func TestDivide(t *testing.T) {
	t.Run("ValidDivision", func(t *testing.T) {
		result, err := Divide(10, 2)
		if err != nil {
			t.Errorf("Unexpected error: %v",
err)
		}
		expected := 5
		if result != expected {
			t.Errorf("Divide(10, 2) = %d; want
%d", result, expected)
```

```
        }
    })


    t.Run("DivisionByZero", func(t *testing.T) {
        _, err := Divide(10, 0)
        if err == nil {
            t.Errorf("Expected an error for
division by zero")
        }
    })
}
```

Step 3: Run the Tests

Execute the tests using:

bash

go test ./calculator

Expected output:

PASS

ok   calculator   0.001s

Benchmarking Performance

Benchmarking measures the performance of specific functions. Go's testing package provides Benchmark functions for this purpose.

Writing a Benchmark Function

1. Benchmark functions start with Benchmark and take a single *testing.B parameter.

2. Use a loop (b.N) to simulate repeated calls.

Example:

go

```go
func BenchmarkAdd(b *testing.B) {
        for i := 0; i < b.N; i++ {
                Add(2, 3)
        }
}
```

Step 1: Add Benchmarks for Calculator Functions

calculator_benchmark_test.go:

go

```go
package calculator
```

```go
import (
        "testing"
)

func BenchmarkAdd(b *testing.B) {
        for i := 0; i < b.N; i++ {
                Add(2, 3)
        }
}

func BenchmarkSubtract(b *testing.B) {
        for i := 0; i < b.N; i++ {
                Subtract(5, 3)
        }
}

func BenchmarkMultiply(b *testing.B) {
        for i := 0; i < b.N; i++ {
                Multiply(4, 5)
        }
}
```

```
func BenchmarkDivide(b *testing.B) {
        for i := 0; i < b.N; i++ {
                Divide(10, 2)
        }
}
```

Step 2: Run the Benchmarks

Run benchmarks using:

bash

go test -bench=.

Example output:

bash

goos: darwin

goarch: amd64

pkg: calculator

BenchmarkAdd-8   1000000000   0.2874 ns/op

BenchmarkSubtract-8   1000000000   0.2901 ns/op

BenchmarkMultiply-8   1000000000   0.2875 ns/op

BenchmarkDivide-8   1000000000   0.3524 ns/op

Table-Driven Tests

Table-driven tests allow testing multiple cases in a single function, reducing duplication.

Example:

go

```
func TestAdd(t *testing.T) {
        tests := []struct {
                a, b, expected int
        }{
                {2, 3, 5},
                {0, 0, 0},
                {-1, -1, -2},
        }

        for _, tt := range tests {
                result := Add(tt.a, tt.b)
                if result != tt.expected {
```

```
            t.Errorf("Add(%d, %d) = %d; want
%d", tt.a, tt.b, result, tt.expected)
            }
        }
}
```

Optimizing Performance

After benchmarking, identify and optimize bottlenecks in your code.

Using Go's Profiler

1. Enable profiling with the -cpuprofile flag:

bash

```
go test -bench=. -cpuprofile=cpu.prof
```

2. Analyze the profile with go tool pprof:

bash

```
go tool pprof cpu.prof
```

3. Use interactive commands (top, list) or generate visualizations:

bash

```
go tool pprof -http=:8080 cpu.prof
```

Advantages of Go's Testing and Benchmarking

1. **Integration with Build Tools**: go test seamlessly integrates with Go's build and CI tools.

2. **Ease of Use**: Minimal boilerplate makes testing and benchmarking straightforward.

3. **Profiling Support**: Built-in profiling tools aid in identifying and resolving performance bottlenecks.

Example: Complete Testing and Benchmarking

1. Implement the calculator module (calculator.go).

2. Write unit tests (calculator_test.go).

3. Write benchmarks (calculator_benchmark_test.go).

4. Run tests and benchmarks:

bash

```
go test ./calculator
```

```
go test -bench=. ./calculator
```

Extending the Example

1. **Integration Tests**
   Test the interaction between multiple functions
   or modules.

2. **Mocking**
   Use mocks to test functions that depend on
   external systems.

3. **Load Testing**
   Use tools like wrk or ab to simulate concurrent
   requests for API endpoints.

4. **Error Injection**
   Simulate errors in benchmarks to evaluate
   system resilience.

This chapter introduced Go's testing and
benchmarking features through the calculator module
example. You learned to write unit tests, run
benchmarks, and optimize performance using
profiling tools. Testing and benchmarking are critical
for delivering reliable and performant applications,
making them essential skills for any Go developer.

Deploying Go Applications

Deployment is a critical step in delivering applications to end users. Go's ability to build static executables and support for cross-compilation make it ideal for deployment across diverse environments. In this chapter, we'll explore building executables, cross-compilation, and deploying a Go web service using Docker and Kubernetes.

Building Executables in Go

Building an Executable

Go compiles programs into standalone executables, making them easy to deploy. To build an executable for your application:

bash

go build -o myapp

- **-o**: Specifies the output file name (myapp in this case).

- The executable contains all necessary dependencies, including the Go runtime.

Running the Executable

Once built, you can run the executable:

bash

```
./myapp
```

Cross-Compilation in Go

Cross-compilation allows building executables for different operating systems and architectures from a single machine.

Specifying Target OS and Architecture

Use the GOOS and GOARCH environment variables to specify the target platform.

Example:

bash

```
# Build for Linux
GOOS=linux GOARCH=amd64 go build -o myapp-linux

# Build for Windows
GOOS=windows GOARCH=amd64 go build -o myapp.exe
```

Common Targets

GOOS	GOARCH	Description
linux	amd64	Linux 64-bit
darwin	arm64	macOS on ARM processors
windows	amd64	Windows 64-bit

Deploying Go Applications with Docker

Docker simplifies application deployment by packaging it into a container along with all dependencies.

Benefits of Docker

1. **Portability**: Containers run consistently across environments.

2. **Isolation**: Containers are isolated from the host system.

3. **Scalability**: Easily scale applications with container orchestration tools like Kubernetes.

Example: Containerizing a Go Web Service

We'll create a simple Go web service, build it into a Docker image, and run it in a container.

Step 1: Create a Go Web Service

main.go:

```go

package main

import (
        "fmt"
        "net/http"
)

func handler(w http.ResponseWriter, r *http.Request) {
        fmt.Fprintf(w, "Hello, Docker!")
}

func main() {
        http.HandleFunc("/", handler)
        fmt.Println("Server is running on port 8080")
        http.ListenAndServe(":8080", nil)
}
```

Build the executable:

bash

```
go build -o webapp
```

Step 2: Write a Dockerfile

Create a Dockerfile to define the container image.

Dockerfile:

dockerfile

```
# Use the official Go image as a builder
FROM golang:1.20 as builder

# Set the working directory
WORKDIR /app

# Copy the Go source files
COPY main.go .

# Build the Go executable
RUN go build -o webapp
```

```
# Use a minimal image for the final container
FROM alpine:latest

# Copy the Go executable from the builder
COPY --from=builder /app/webapp /webapp

# Expose the application port
EXPOSE 8080

# Run the application
CMD ["/webapp"]
```

Step 3: Build the Docker Image

Build the Docker image:

bash

```
docker build -t go-webapp .
```

Step 4: Run the Docker Container

Run the container:

bash

```
docker run -p 8080:8080 go-webapp
```

- **-p 8080:8080**: Maps port 8080 on the host to port 8080 in the container.

Visit http://localhost:8080 to see the message:

```
Hello, Docker!
```

Deploying Go Applications with Kubernetes

Kubernetes is a container orchestration platform that automates deployment, scaling, and management of containerized applications.

Example: Deploying the Go Web Service with Kubernetes

We'll deploy the Dockerized Go web service to a Kubernetes cluster.

Step 1: Create a Kubernetes Deployment

deployment.yaml:

yaml

```
apiVersion: apps/v1
```

```yaml
kind: Deployment
metadata:
  name: go-webapp
spec:
  replicas: 2
  selector:
    matchLabels:
      app: go-webapp
  template:
    metadata:
      labels:
        app: go-webapp
    spec:
      containers:
      - name: go-webapp
        image: go-webapp:latest
        ports:
        - containerPort: 8080
```

- **replicas**: Specifies the number of pods to run.
- **image**: The Docker image for the web service.

Step 2: Create a Kubernetes Service

service.yaml:

yaml

apiVersion: v1

kind: Service

metadata:

  name: go-webapp-service

spec:

  type: LoadBalancer

  selector:

    app: go-webapp

  ports:

  - protocol: TCP

    port: 80

    targetPort: 8080

- **type: LoadBalancer**: Exposes the service externally.

Step 3: Deploy to Kubernetes

1. **Apply the Deployment and Service**

bash

```bash
kubectl apply -f deployment.yaml

kubectl apply -f service.yaml
```

2. **Check Deployment Status**

```bash
kubectl get deployments

kubectl get pods

kubectl get services
```

3. **Access the Service**
   - Use the external IP of the service to access the application.

Best Practices for Deploying Go Applications

1. **Static Builds**
   Use CGO_ENABLED=0 for static binaries:

```bash
CGO_ENABLED=0 GOOS=linux GOARCH=amd64
go build -o myapp
```

2. **Minimal Base Images**
   Use lightweight images like alpine for smaller container sizes.

3. **Environment Variables**
   Use environment variables to configure your application.

4. **Health Checks**
   Add health check endpoints to monitor application status.

5. **Scalability**
   Use Kubernetes to manage scaling and load balancing.

Advanced Deployment Options

1. **Continuous Integration/Continuous Deployment (CI/CD)**
   Automate builds, tests, and deployments with tools like GitHub Actions, GitLab CI, or Jenkins.

2. **Cloud Services**
   Deploy to platforms like AWS, Google Cloud, or Azure using their container services.

3. **Service Mesh**
   Integrate a service mesh like Istio for advanced traffic management and monitoring.

This chapter covered building executables, cross-compilation, and deploying Go applications with Docker and Kubernetes. The example of containerizing and deploying a Go web service demonstrated the power of these tools in delivering robust and scalable applications. In the next chapter, we'll explore optimizing Go applications for performance and debugging.

Optimizing for Performance in Go

Performance is a critical aspect of modern applications, especially in systems requiring real-time processing or handling large-scale data. Go's design emphasizes speed and simplicity, but further optimization often requires careful coding, debugging, and profiling. This chapter explores techniques for writing efficient Go code, introduces debugging and profiling tools like pprof and trace, and demonstrates optimization through a video processing pipeline example.

Tips for Writing Efficient Go Code

1. Use Efficient Data Structures

Choosing the right data structure can significantly impact performance:

- Use slices instead of arrays for flexibility and dynamic sizing.

- Prefer maps for fast key-value lookups.

- Avoid excessive use of pointers unless necessary to reduce memory overhead.

2. Optimize Loops

Minimize work inside loops by:

- Reducing function calls within the loop.

- Using precomputed values where possible.
  Example:

go

```
// Suboptimal
for i := 0; i < len(items); i++ {
    process(items[i])
}
```

```
// Optimal
n := len(items)
for i := 0; i < n; i++ {
    process(items[i])
}
```

3. Avoid Premature Allocation

Allocate only the memory you need. Over-allocating can waste resources:

go

```
// Suboptimal
```

```
data := make([]int, 1000000) // Large allocation
upfront
```

```
// Optimal
```

```
data := []int{} // Grow dynamically as needed
```

4. Leverage Goroutines and Channels

Go's concurrency model allows efficient parallel processing. Use goroutines and channels for tasks like I/O or CPU-intensive computations.

5. Profile Before Optimizing

Always profile your code to identify bottlenecks before attempting optimizations. Optimizing without data can lead to wasted effort.

Debugging and Profiling Tools

Go provides built-in tools for profiling and tracing to help identify performance bottlenecks.

1. pprof

pprof is a profiling tool that collects performance data, such as CPU usage, memory allocation, and goroutine activity.

CPU Profiling

1. **Enable CPU Profiling**: Add the following code to enable profiling:

```go
import (
    "log"
    "os"
    "runtime/pprof"
)

func main() {
    f, err := os.Create("cpu.prof")
    if err != nil {
        log.Fatal(err)
    }
    pprof.StartCPUProfile(f)
    defer pprof.StopCPUProfile()

    // Your program logic here
}
```

2. **Run the Program**:

```bash
```

```
go run main.go
```

3. **Analyze the Profile**: Use pprof to analyze the generated profile:

```bash
```

```
go tool pprof cpu.prof
```

4. **Interactive Commands**:
   - top: Shows functions consuming the most CPU.
   - list: Displays the source code with time annotations.

---

2. trace

trace provides detailed runtime tracing, including goroutine activity, system calls, and garbage collection.

1. **Enable Tracing**:

```go
```

```go
import (
    "log"
    "os"
    "runtime/trace"
```

```go
)

func main() {
    f, err := os.Create("trace.out")
    if err != nil {
        log.Fatal(err)
    }
    defer f.Close()

    trace.Start(f)
    defer trace.Stop()

    // Your program logic here
}
```

2. **Run the Program**:

bash

```bash
go run main.go
```

3. **Analyze the Trace**:

bash

```bash
go tool trace trace.out
```

Example: Profiling and Optimizing a Video Processing Pipeline

Step 1: Define the Problem

A video processing pipeline performs the following tasks:

1. Decoding video frames.

2. Applying a filter to each frame.

3. Encoding processed frames into a new video file.

The goal is to optimize the pipeline for performance using profiling and code adjustments.

Step 2: Initial Implementation

video_pipeline.go:

go

```
package main

import (
        "fmt"
        "time"
```

```go
)

type Frame struct {
	ID int
}


func decodeFrames(total int) []Frame {
	frames := make([]Frame, total)
	for i := 0; i < total; i++ {
		time.Sleep(10 * time.Millisecond) // Simulate decoding time
		frames[i] = Frame{ID: i}
	}
	return frames
}


func applyFilter(frame Frame) Frame {
	time.Sleep(5 * time.Millisecond) // Simulate filter time
	frame.ID += 1000
	return frame
}
```

```go
func encodeFrames(frames []Frame) {
    for _, frame := range frames {
        time.Sleep(10 * time.Millisecond) // Simulate encoding time
        fmt.Printf("Encoded frame %d\n", frame.ID)
    }
}

func main() {
    totalFrames := 100

    // Step 1: Decode frames
    frames := decodeFrames(totalFrames)

    // Step 2: Apply filter
    for i, frame := range frames {
        frames[i] = applyFilter(frame)
    }

    // Step 3: Encode frames
    encodeFrames(frames)
}
```

Run the program:

bash

```
go run video_pipeline.go
```

Step 3: Profile the Pipeline

1. Add CPU profiling:

go

```
f, err := os.Create("cpu.prof")
if err != nil {
    log.Fatal(err)
}
pprof.StartCPUProfile(f)
defer pprof.StopCPUProfile()
```

2. Analyze the profile:

bash

```
go tool pprof cpu.prof
```

3. Output (example):

css

Showing top 10 nodes out of 20

```
flat flat%  sum%      cum  cum%
200ms 40.00% 40.00%   400ms 80.00%
main.decodeFrames
100ms 20.00% 60.00%   200ms 40.00%
main.applyFilter
```

Step 4: Optimize the Pipeline

Optimization 1: Parallelize Frame Processing

Use goroutines to process frames concurrently:

go

```go
func applyFilterConcurrent(frames []Frame) []Frame {
    ch := make(chan Frame, len(frames))

    for _, frame := range frames {
        go func(f Frame) {
            ch <- applyFilter(f)
        }(frame)
    }

    processed := make([]Frame, len(frames))
    for i := range frames {
```

```
        processed[i] = <-ch

    }

    return processed

}
```

Optimization 2: Adjust Memory Allocation

Preallocate memory for slices to avoid repeated allocations:

go

```
frames := make([]Frame, totalFrames)
```

Step 5: Reprofile the Optimized Code

1. Rerun the optimized program with profiling enabled.

2. Compare results:

css

```
Showing top 10 nodes out of 20

flat  flat%  sum%      cum   cum%

100ms  25.00%  25.00%    250ms  62.50%
main.decodeFrames
```

50ms   12.50% 37.50%   150ms 37.50%
main.applyFilterConcurrent

Best Practices for Optimization

1. **Minimize Memory Allocations**
   Reuse memory where possible by using object
   pools or preallocating slices.

2. **Reduce Lock Contention**
   Minimize the use of shared resources to avoid
   contention in concurrent programs.

3. **Profile Regularly**
   Profile code after every significant change to
   ensure optimizations are effective.

4. **Leverage Concurrency**
   Use goroutines and channels to parallelize I/O-
   bound or CPU-intensive tasks.

This chapter demonstrated techniques for optimizing
Go applications, including profiling with pprof, tracing
with trace, and implementing targeted optimizations.
The example of the video processing pipeline
highlighted how to identify bottlenecks and improve
performance using parallel processing and memory
adjustments. With these tools and techniques, you
can build highly efficient Go applications tailored to
demanding use cases.

Conclusion

Real-World Use Cases and Future Trends in Go

Go has established itself as a powerful language for building scalable, efficient, and maintainable applications. Its simplicity, performance, and concurrency model make it a top choice for various industries, including cloud computing, microservices, and DevOps. In this chapter, we'll explore real-world use cases, discuss the future of Go and its ecosystem, and conclude with a final project that integrates the language's key features.

Real-World Use Cases of Go

1. Cloud Computing and Distributed Systems

- **Case Study: Kubernetes**
  Kubernetes, the most popular container orchestration system, is written in Go. Its modular architecture and focus on performance benefit from Go's concurrency model, making it capable of managing thousands of containers across distributed systems.

- **Why Go?**
    - Efficient concurrency via goroutines and channels.
    - Strong standard library for networking and HTTP.
    - Ease of deployment with static binaries.

2. Microservices

- **Case Study: Uber**
Uber rewrote many of its critical services in Go to achieve lower latency and higher throughput. Go's simplicity and performance made it possible to handle billions of API calls daily.

- **Why Go?**
    - Lightweight frameworks (e.g., Gin, Echo) for microservices.
    - Built-in profiling tools for performance optimization.
    - Easy-to-understand syntax and minimal runtime overhead.

3. DevOps and Automation

- **Case Study: Docker**
Docker, the tool that revolutionized containerization, is also written in Go. Its lightweight binaries and fast execution make it ideal for DevOps workflows.

- **Why Go?**

  - Static binaries simplify deployment in containerized environments.

  - Strong support for CLI tools and system-level programming.

  - High performance and scalability.

4. Real-Time Systems

- **Case Study: Twitch**
  Twitch uses Go for real-time chat systems, handling millions of concurrent users. The language's concurrency and low-latency capabilities enable Twitch to scale efficiently.

- **Why Go?**

  - Efficient handling of high-concurrency use cases.

  - Built-in garbage collection optimized for low-latency operations.

  - Support for WebSocket and streaming protocols.

The Future of Go and Its Ecosystem

1. Trends Shaping Go's Adoption

1. **Growing Cloud-Native Adoption**
   Go continues to dominate the cloud-native ecosystem with projects like Kubernetes, Prometheus, and Helm. Its features align well with cloud-native principles such as scalability and modularity.

2. **WebAssembly and Edge Computing**
   Go's support for WebAssembly (Wasm) enables it to run lightweight applications at the edge. This trend is expected to grow as edge computing becomes more critical.

3. **Enhanced Tooling and IDE Support**
   The Go ecosystem is evolving with better tools for debugging, testing, and profiling. Tools like Delve and integration with modern IDEs ensure a smoother developer experience.

4. **AI and Machine Learning**
   While not traditionally associated with AI, Go's simplicity and performance make it a candidate for developing scalable AI services, especially when integrated with cloud-based ML platforms.

2. Upcoming Features in Go

1. **Generics**
   The introduction of generics in Go 1.18 was a

significant milestone, enabling more reusable and type-safe code. The community is actively exploring best practices for leveraging this feature.

2. **Improved Error Handling**
   Go's focus on explicit error handling is evolving with discussions around improving the ergonomics of error reporting.

3. **Increased Ecosystem Support**
   New frameworks and libraries are continuously being developed, expanding Go's reach into domains like machine learning, game development, and financial systems.

Final Project: Building an End-to-End Application

To consolidate the concepts learned in this book, let's build a final project: a **Task Management Platform** that integrates Go's features, including web development, concurrency, and database interaction.

Step 1: Define the Requirements

The platform will:

1. Provide a web interface to manage tasks.

2. Allow users to:

   o Create tasks.

- List all tasks.
- Mark tasks as completed.
- Delete tasks.
3. Use SQLite for persistent storage.
4. Include a REST API for external integrations.

Step 2: Plan the Architecture

1. **Frontend**
   - Serve HTML pages using Go's html/template.
2. **Backend**
   - Expose REST endpoints for task operations.
3. **Database**
   - Use SQLite for storing tasks persistently.
4. **Concurrency**
   - Handle task creation and updates in parallel.

Step 3: Implementation

1. Directory Structure

go

```
task-manager/
├── main.go
├── handlers/
│   ├── api.go
│   ├── web.go
├── templates/
│   ├── index.html
├── database/
│   └── database.go
├── models/
│   └── task.go
```

---

2. Code

main.go: Entry Point

go

```
package main

import (
```

```go
        "log"

        "net/http"

        "task-manager/handlers"

        "task-manager/database"
)

func main() {
        // Initialize database
        err := database.InitDB("tasks.db")
        if err != nil {
                log.Fatalf("Failed to initialize database: %v", err)
        }

        // Routes
        http.HandleFunc("/", handlers.WebIndex)
        http.HandleFunc("/api/tasks", handlers.APITasks)

        // Start server
        log.Println("Server running on http://localhost:8080")
        http.ListenAndServe(":8080", nil)
```

```
}
```

---

database/database.go: Database Initialization

go

```go
package database

import (
        "database/sql"
        "log"

        _ "modernc.org/sqlite"
)

var DB *sql.DB

func InitDB(filepath string) error {
        var err error
        DB, err = sql.Open("sqlite", filepath)
        if err != nil {
                return err
        }
```

```go
	// Create tasks table
	_, err = DB.Exec(`
	CREATE TABLE IF NOT EXISTS tasks (
		id INTEGER PRIMARY KEY AUTOINCREMENT,
		title TEXT NOT NULL,
		completed BOOLEAN NOT NULL
	)`)
	if err != nil {
		return err
	}

	log.Println("Database initialized")
	return nil
}
```

---

handlers/web.go: Web Handlers

go

```go
package handlers
```

```go
import (

    "html/template"

    "net/http"

    "task-manager/models"

)


func WebIndex(w http.ResponseWriter, r *http.Request) {

    tasks, err := models.GetTasks()

    if err != nil {

        http.Error(w, "Unable to fetch tasks", http.StatusInternalServerError)

        return

    }


    tmpl, _ := template.ParseFiles("templates/index.html")

    tmpl.Execute(w, tasks)

}
```

---

handlers/api.go: REST API Handlers

go

```go
package handlers

import (
        "encoding/json"

        "net/http"

        "task-manager/models"
)


func APITasks(w http.ResponseWriter, r *http.Request) {
        switch r.Method {
        case http.MethodGet:
                tasks, _ := models.GetTasks()
                json.NewEncoder(w).Encode(tasks)
        case http.MethodPost:
                var task models.Task

                json.NewDecoder(r.Body).Decode(&task)
                models.AddTask(task)
                w.WriteHeader(http.StatusCreated)
        default:
                http.Error(w, "Method not allowed",
http.StatusMethodNotAllowed)
```

```go
        }
}
```

---

models/task.go: Task Model

go

```go
package models

import (
        "task-manager/database"
)

type Task struct {
        ID       int    `json:"id"`
        Title    string `json:"title"`
        Completed bool   `json:"completed"`
}

func GetTasks() ([]Task, error) {
        rows, err := database.DB.Query("SELECT id, title, completed FROM tasks")
        if err != nil {
```

```go
		return nil, err
	}
	defer rows.Close()

	var tasks []Task
	for rows.Next() {
		var task Task
		rows.Scan(&task.ID, &task.Title, &task.Completed)
		tasks = append(tasks, task)
	}
	return tasks, nil
}


func AddTask(task Task) error {
	_, err := database.DB.Exec("INSERT INTO tasks (title, completed) VALUES (?, ?)", task.Title, false)

	return err
}
```

---

templates/index.html: Frontend Template

html

```html
<!DOCTYPE html>
<html>
<head>
  <title>Task Manager</title>
</head>
<body>
  <h1>Tasks</h1>
  <ul>
    {{range .}}
    <li>{{.Title}} - {{if .Completed}}Completed{{else}}Pending{{end}}</li>
    {{end}}
  </ul>
  <form action="/api/tasks" method="POST">
    <input type="text" name="title" placeholder="New Task" required>
    <button type="submit">Add Task</button>
  </form>
</body>
</html>
```

Step 4: Run and Test

1. **Start the Server**:

bash

```
go run main.go
```

2. **Access the Web Interface**:
   Visit http://localhost:8080.

3. **Test the REST API**:

bash

```
curl -X GET http://localhost:8080/api/tasks
```

This chapter demonstrated real-world use cases of Go, explored its future trends, and culminated with a final project integrating Go's key features. By building the task management platform, you applied skills like web development, database interaction, and REST API design, providing a solid foundation for tackling complex, real-world projects.

www.ingramcontent.com/pod-product-compliance
Lightning Source LLC
LaVergne TN
LVHW022339060326
832902LV00022B/4131